CW01667262

JOHN HOUSTON

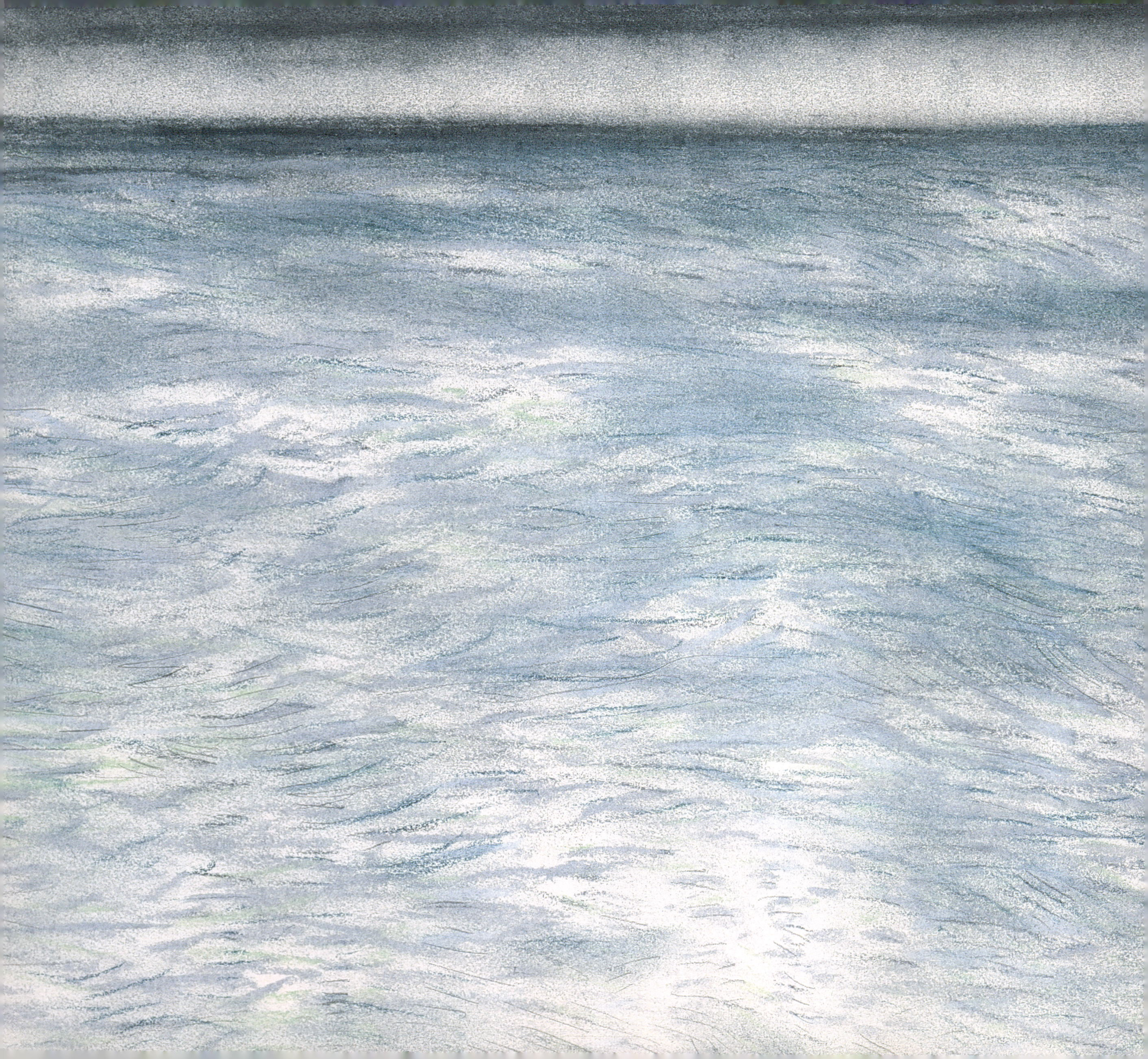

Philip Long

John **Houston**

National Galleries of Scotland
Edinburgh · 2005

Published by the Trustees of the
National Galleries of Scotland for the
exhibition *John Houston* held at the Scottish
National Gallery of Modern Art from
29 September to 13 November 2005.

ISBN 1 903278 72 4

Designed and typeset in Shaker by Dalrymple
Printed in Belgium by Die Keure

Cover: *The Bay after the Storm,* 1988 [no.41]
Frontispiece: detail from *Sea after Rain,* 2002
[no.53]

Foreword

John Houston has contributed greatly to Scottish art over the last half-century, through his own work and his long commitment as a teacher to several generations of students at Edinburgh College of Art. This book, and the exhibition it accompanies, acknowledges that achievement in the year of the artist's seventy-fifth birthday, which we are delighted to celebrate in this way. Houston is a prodigious worker, having held regular exhibitions of his new paintings since the outset of his professional career some fifty years ago. Perhaps as a consequence of the demand for his art, there have been few opportunities to examine a selection of it from across the whole of the artist's career. This retrospective is, therefore, timely and the Scottish National Gallery of Modern Art's organisation of it is indebted to John Houston, who has offered his continual support and has happily agreed to our request for many loans from his own collection. We are very grateful indeed to him and to his wife, Elizabeth. Our sincere gratitude extends to the other lenders, who have parted with a selection of the artist's most important works. We must also thank Guy Peploe and Robin McClure of The Scottish Gallery for their support and advice. We are delighted that the exhibition has been sponsored by Johnston Press. Their generosity has made it possible.

Sir Timothy Clifford
Director-General, National Galleries of Scotland

Richard Calvocoressi
Director, Scottish National Gallery of Modern Art

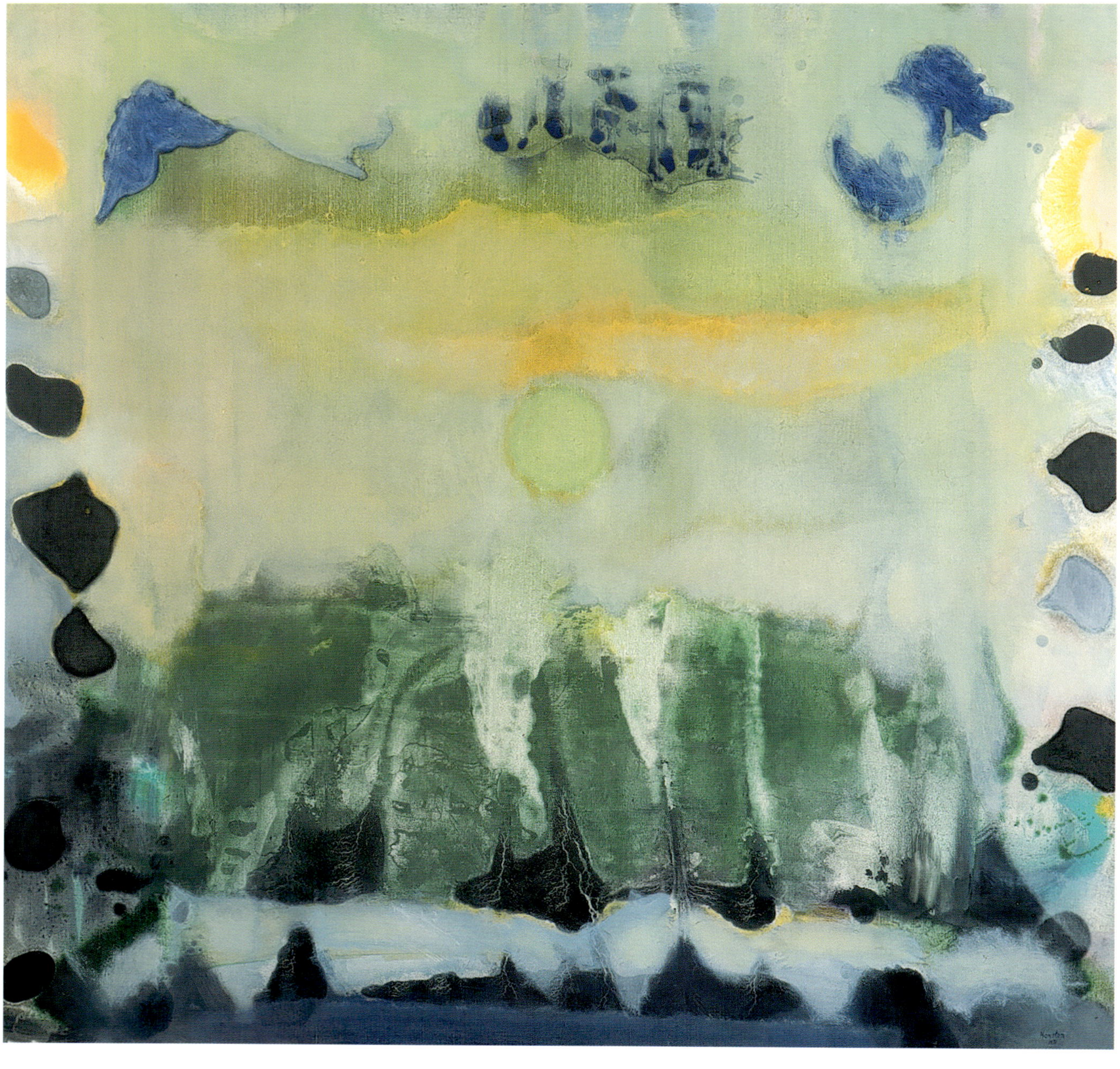

Introduction

John Houston was born in Fife and he grew up in Windygates, on the east coast of Scotland. In the 1950s he settled permanently in Edinburgh, and while he has become a great traveller, the land- and seascape of his home country remain his predominant subject. His painting has been described as expressive, in that it shares with artists such as Edvard Munch and Emil Nolde (whom Houston acknowledges as particular influences) a frequently gestural technique which shows not only the manner in which the paint was applied, but also something of the feelings of the artist. For Houston, these are not the emotions born from the inner neurosis of a painter such as Munch, nor are they the sort of statements made by Nolde, which have been described as expressing something particular to that artist's native Germany. Rather, as becomes clear in the interview with the artist that follows, the driving stimulus for Houston's art derives foremost from his direct experience of nature, which he records in all its variety and reinterprets in his studio.

In some of the most ambitious paintings included here, the group of large land- and seascapes dating from the 1980s onwards, Houston treats the same subject, a particular area of the Scottish east coast, in such differing ways that each painting might be said to have a different emotional character. In the way that the changing mood of a person can be more sympathetically understood through familiarity and intimacy, Houston finds the best subjects for his pictures are ones that are well known to him (hence the preponderance of Scottish subjects), or those he has been able to return to after having had time to reflect upon and judge their character (as has been the case with his interest in Japan). Armed with this knowledge, he is able to work with a greater creative freedom, allowing him to experiment with different approaches or, as he puts it, 'hang different ideas' on his chosen subject.

Yet, as also becomes clear, Houston does not base his work only on his observation of nature. During the process of their making, his paintings take on an independent life. This comes about as a result of the artist's intuitive response as to how a picture should develop once it is underway, most particularly at a point when, in his opinion, the work appears to have become too planned. Houston describes this as 'losing his temper' with the picture and he relies on the energy this creates to help him bring back something of the mood which he first experienced in front of his chosen motif. The retention of that original feeling is constantly striven for above any truthful likeness to the subject, and he freely changes his composition to help him achieve this.

Important too, is the continuing influence of his art-college education and of other formative experiences. As an artist who was educated in Scotland, Houston's early development is fascinating. It has been said that in twentieth-century Scottish painting, two particular tendencies can be identified, that of the hard-lined, illusionistic style practised by Glasgow-trained artists such as James Cowie, Edward

opposite: Sea Sounds, 1971
Artist's collection · no.28

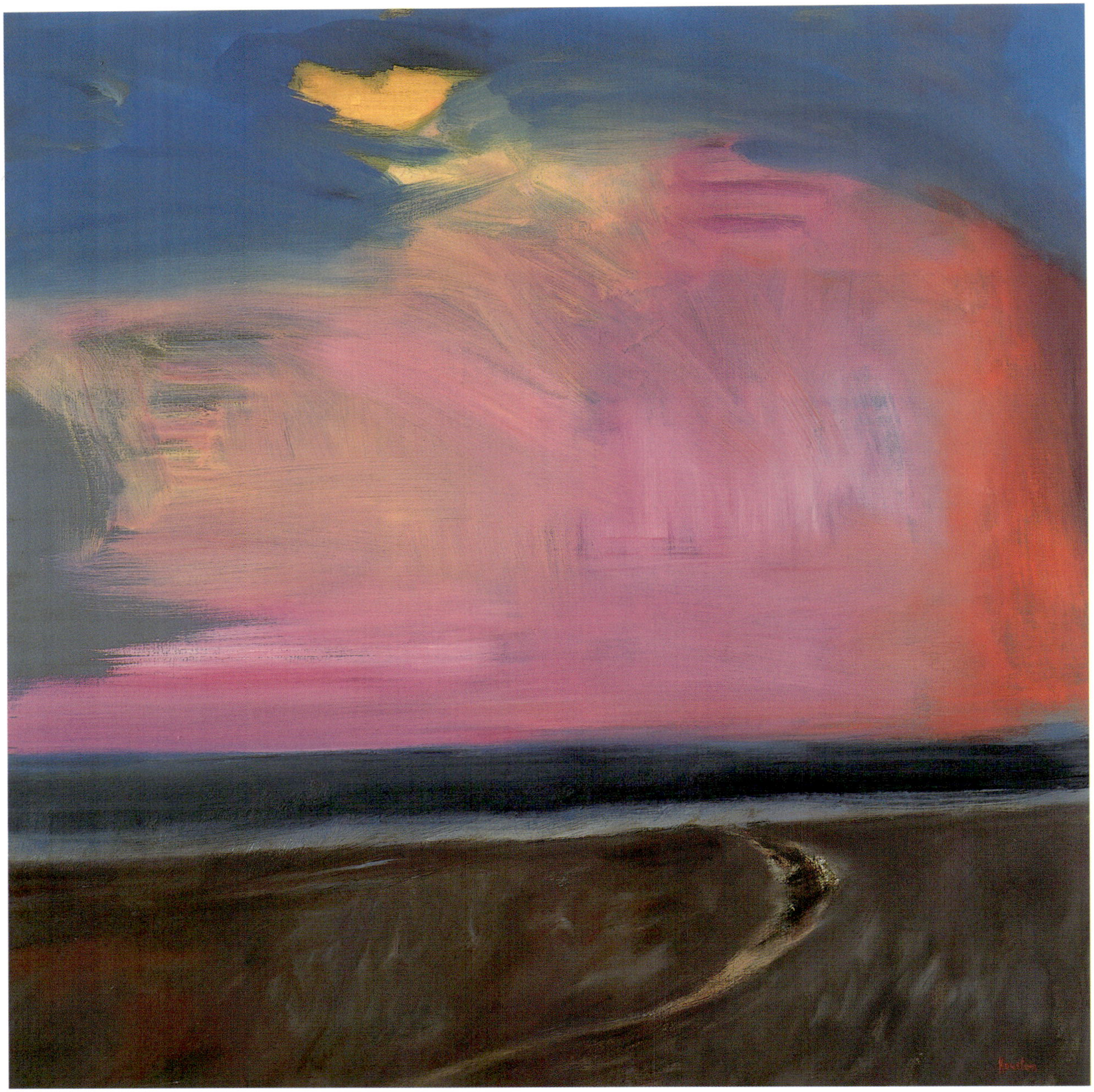

Baird and James McIntosh Patrick; and the more intuitive and expressionistic approach of those such as William Gillies and William MacTaggart, who are so strongly associated with Edinburgh and who were a direct influence on the young Houston. Faced with his expressive style and bold colour, it may be tempting to classify Houston's painting as part of the latter tradition, but for him such a simple distinction is not possible: 'I have never thought of the different traditions coming from Glasgow and Edinburgh. There were artists in both cities working in these directions; it wasn't clear one way or other.'

This is borne out by the tuition the artist received in the late 1940s from Robert Henderson Blyth, who had studied at Glasgow and then under Cowie at Hospitalfield at Arbroath, before taking up a teaching post at Edinburgh College of Art. Blyth introduced his students to a methodical approach to picture construction which has affected Houston's art ever since. Even in his most exuberantly worked paintings, Houston imposes an order through the use of a simple but clearly defined compositional structure. Since the 1980s this has most commonly taken the form of a strong horizon line, perhaps combined with a sweeping curve representing the line of the shore. This is a method of containment, of providing a focus, which for Houston stops the painting 'collapsing' or turning into 'loose bits of paint'. The desire to have an underlying order based on the natural world, but at the same time experimenting with abstraction, can be traced right through the artist's professional career. While in Italy during his scholarship year, begun in 1953, his interest in the Italian landscape became greater as its topography was revealed under winter conditions. Sixteen years later, while in the United States, he was able to study post-war American art in depth, after which he completed works such as *Golden Lake II* and *Sea Sounds*, which share something of Abstract Expressionism's interest in unstructured picture space. During the 1970s, faced with conceptual art, he gradually resolved the crisis he felt as a near-abstract painter by working in an increasingly figurative manner. This was aided by a choice of a landscape motifs – such as the cliffs at Les Petites-Dalles – of such strong geological form that they re-imposed an order in his painting.

Since that point Houston has worked with a constant energy, experimenting with figure subjects and still life alongside his constant preoccupation with landscape. In one of these, *Path to the Sea*, completed in 2003, the broad, alternating brush-strokes are applied in such a way that they seem to go beyond representation, becoming, instead, a painterly equivalent of the radiant sky that first moved the artist. Houston's personality is one of considerable modesty and an even temperament, so it may be surprising to read of the frustration he can feel during the process of painting. The duration of his career and the command he demonstrates in such recent works might suggest he is at ease with his art but, as is shown, while he is able to give some order to the creative method he follows, much also depends on his dissatisfaction with what he has done to allow him to move on. In discussing his experience, he does so with a deepness of memory and a conviction for art which give us not only an insight into the recent cultural history of Scotland, but also into the process of creativity itself.

Philip Long

opposite: Path to the Sea, 2002–3
Private collection · no.55

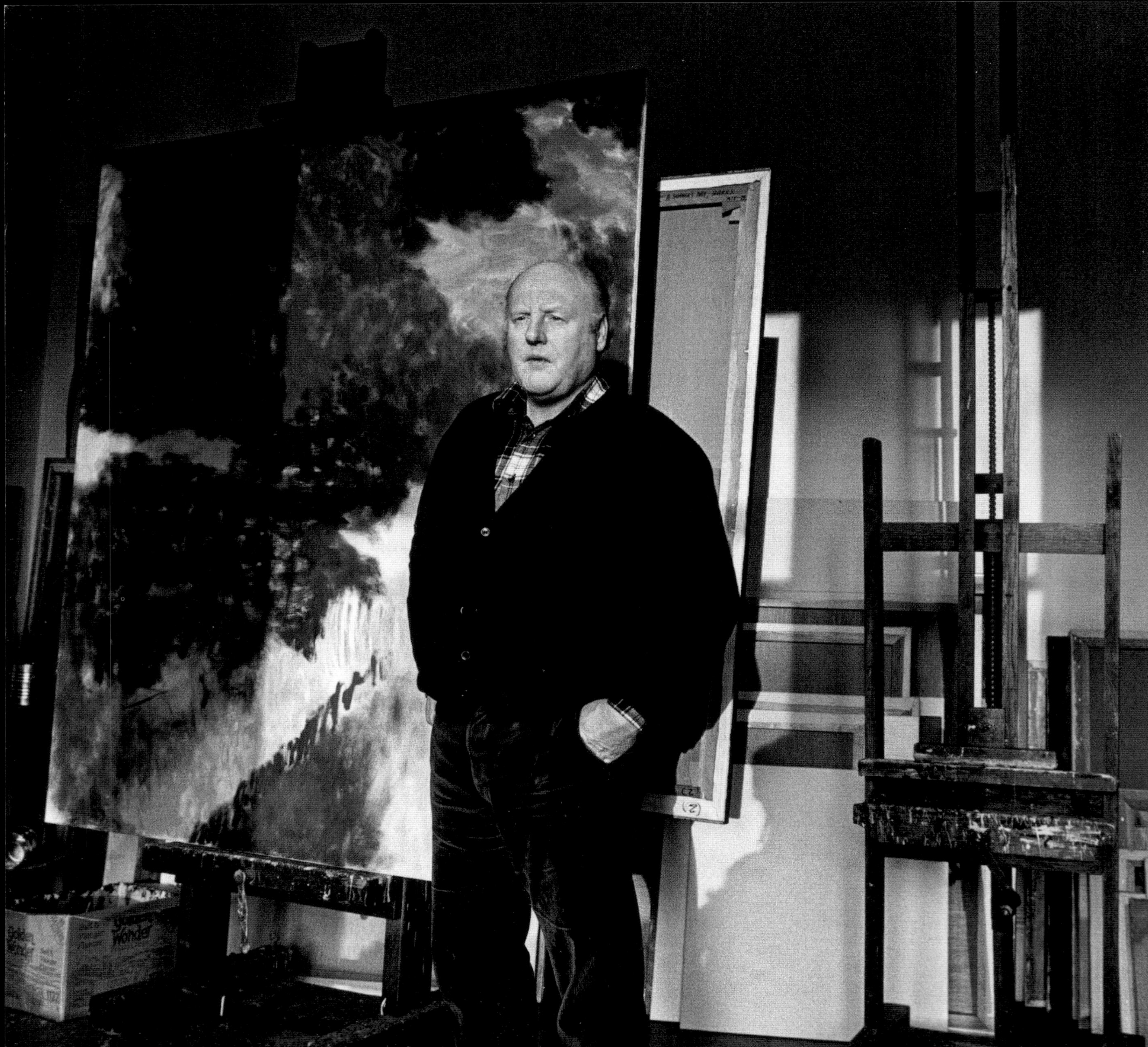
Golden Wonder

John Houston in conversation with Philip Long

— *Philip Long: Can you tell me about growing up in Fife and how your interest in painting developed?*

John Houston: I grew up with my father's family in Windygates, where my grand-parents had run the hotel since 1904. They were originally from Markinch, where my grandfather had the Galloway Inn. Windygates was a big operation, and they were all mad about horses. There were huge stables at the back, so not only were they running the hotel, they also ran the local coal merchants, delivered materials for the gas works and all sorts of other things. In the early days some of the older sons took customers from one hotel to the next by pony and trap. One of my uncles had been in the cavalry during the First World War, so I was taught to ride cavalry style. A great deal of my early life was spent riding, and going to horse sales and races all over the country. That was one side of my youth; the other side was sport. My cousin was a professional footballer with Hearts and Arsenal and I was very keen on football, as well as cricket, tennis and running. I was quite fast when I was young. That's another lifetime away!

— *You played football professionally, didn't you?*

Yes I did, later on, in 1951 when I was a student I played for Dundee United, but only for a year. I had a very bad knee injury and that finished that. The art started at the end of primary school. We didn't have an art teacher, but once every few months the head art teacher from Buckhaven High School came around all the primary schools in the area. He was called Robert Morris, and had been a contemporary of William Gillies. They had shown together in London in the 1920s. Morris had been at Edinburgh College of Art and was a pilot in the First World War. He started teaching at Buckhaven High School in the early 1930s. A lot of his students went to Edinburgh College of Art. The earliest one, I think, was William Gear in the early 1930s.

— *You began at Edinburgh College of Art after the Second World War, when William Gillies was head of the School of Drawing and Painting. Can you tell me your first impressions of the college?*

Yes, I started in 1948 and there were a lot of ex-war people there, for example James

John Houston in his studio
photograph by Peter Cattrell, 1981
Artist's collection

Cumming and Robin Philipson, who had just started teaching. Their training was interrupted by the war, like Gillies's during the First World War. So there you were, a little boy from school, surrounded by these men in flying kit and other bits of uniform, who made quite an impression. They had a very lively affect on the college because they were used to making their own entertainment. They had created societies in the forces or, in some cases, prisoner-of-war camps, but they also worked very hard. Gillies was always around. He visited every class now and again and if he couldn't say something constructive, helpful or encouraging, he just walked on. It was at the college I first met my long-time friend, David Michie.

— *Did Gillies have any particular teaching methods?*

No, no particular methods. His was very much an intuitive response. He obviously had strong opinions, which I began to find out about later when I was a teacher under him; then it became clear he had a fair idea who were the interesting people in the college. I remember in my first year teaching, the importance of keeping your eyes open and listening to what the others were saying. I can recollect, for example, my colleague, John Busby, saying, 'I've got an interesting guy in the first year called John Bellany.'

— *Did other teachers have a particular impact?*

Oh yes. I suppose the one person who made the biggest earliest impact in my first year of painting was Robert Henderson Blyth. Penelope Beaton was also a very supportive and encouraging teacher, both at college and in the first years after being a student. In fact, I went to college to do design. I was going to be a stained glass artist and mural painter.

— *Was that a vocation or a conscious decision that it would help you into a job?*

It seemed interesting to do, but in the course of the first year, painting began to take over and I was fortunate that in my year there were a number of interesting painters. At school, even within a big art department, most either went on to become architects, or it was just a subject people did before they went on to something else. Henderson Blyth was always very supportive. His great hero was James Cowie. He taught Cowie's method of painting, which was making sketches first, which would then be coloured and squared up before applying oil; it was quite a strict way of doing things.

— *Were there particular subjects imposed, alongside that rigorous method of doing things?*

Not really. The only time a subject was given was at the end-of-year tests. There was a composition test, drawing test and so on. For the composition test, there were usually two or three titles, fairly broad titles, like 'circus' or 'workers'. Before that you were allowed to paint anything. I started painting the things around me at home in Windygates, where there was a lot of opencast mining going on, as well as

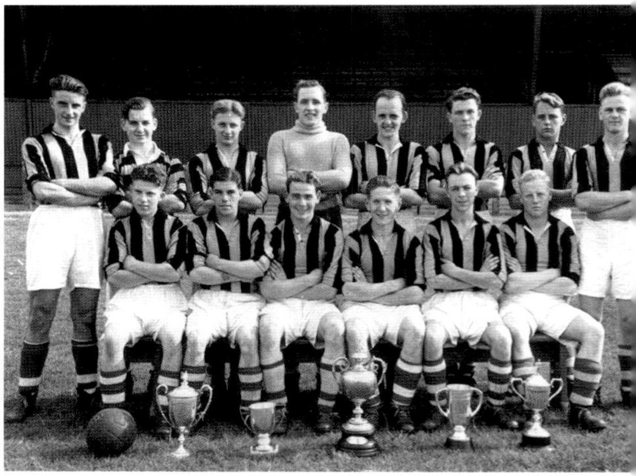

right: Houston (front row, far right) in Bayview Youth Club U21 Football Team, c.1948
Artist's collection

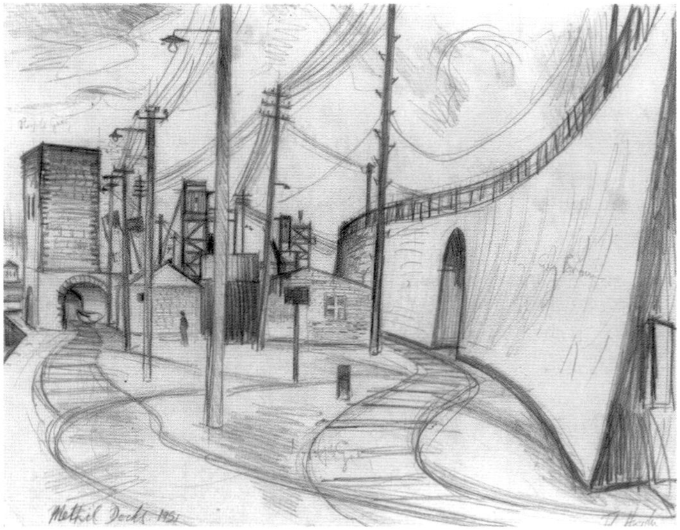

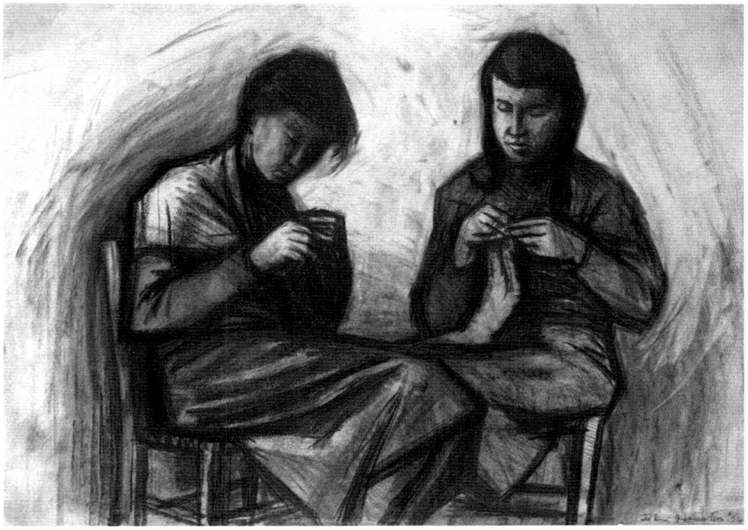

left: Methil Docks, 1951
Artist's collection

right: Two Italian Girls Knitting, Anticoli, 1954
Artist's collection · no.20

farming and the work of the distilleries and the docks. My mother's family had a small stevedore business, with about twelve men who unloaded wood from ships at Methil Docks and then filled them up with coal to take back to the Baltic ports. I was often taken to the docks as a small boy, and later as a student I drew the coal pits and miners and things like that. My mother's family were also mad about flowers; her father was a great gardener and well-known judge at flower shows in the area.

— *Some of your first works were of industrial scenes, not a common subject in art in Scotland at that time.*

Henderson Blyth made pictures of men working in the streets around Edinburgh. But more generally at that time there was a movement among art students in Britain towards this kind of realism. We were seeing a similar thing in Italian films, in particular in De Sica's *The Bicycle Thief* and Rossellini's *Open City*, which made quite an impression. We took part in young contemporary exhibitions, where the paintings were chosen by the college staff and sent to London. Few of us went down to see them, but we saw the catalogues or occasionally our names would appear in the reviews. In one, the names mentioned were Frank Auerbach, John Bratby and John Houston! The subjects were often workers

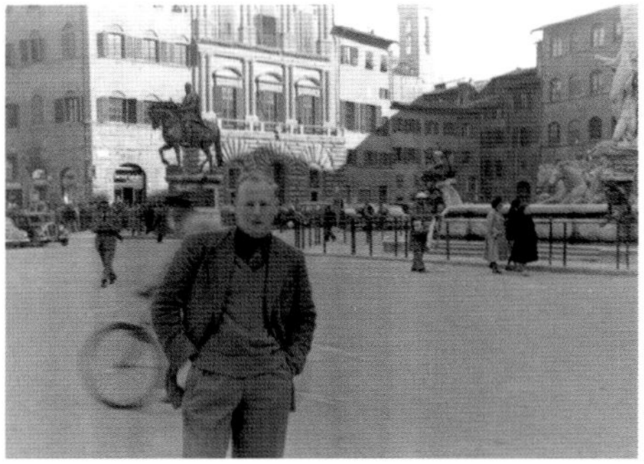

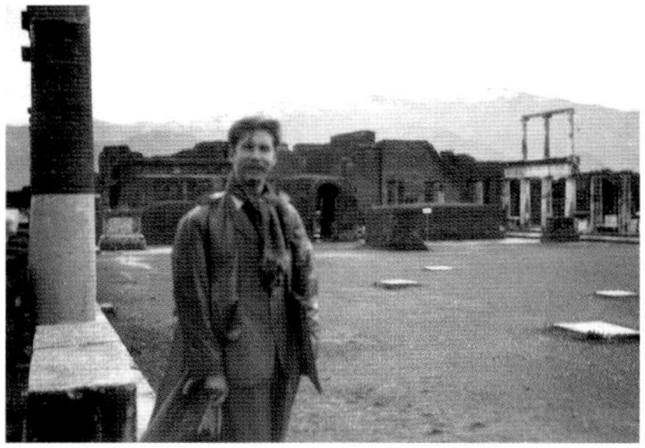

far left: John Houston in Florence, 1953
Artist's collection

left: David Michie at Pompeii, 1954
Artist's collection

below: David Michie in Florence, 1953
Artist's collection

and industrial landscapes. One of the first exhibitions I was included in, which was seen across Europe, was a commission from Shell Petroleum, who sent artists to sites all over Europe. We had to paint tankers, Shell buildings and so on; I painted a refinery. There were a few artists who were doing that sort of thing – Prunella Clough and Keith Vaughan – making paintings of people who were working.

— *How aware were you of those artists and that type of work at the time?*

When I went to college in 1948 the library was half empty, and the books that were there were pre-war. The first new books that arrived were a series by Penguin, the Modern Masters series. One of them was on Henry Moore and featured his drawings of miners and people sleeping underground during the Blitz; they were influential. Ben Shahn and Edward Hopper were the two

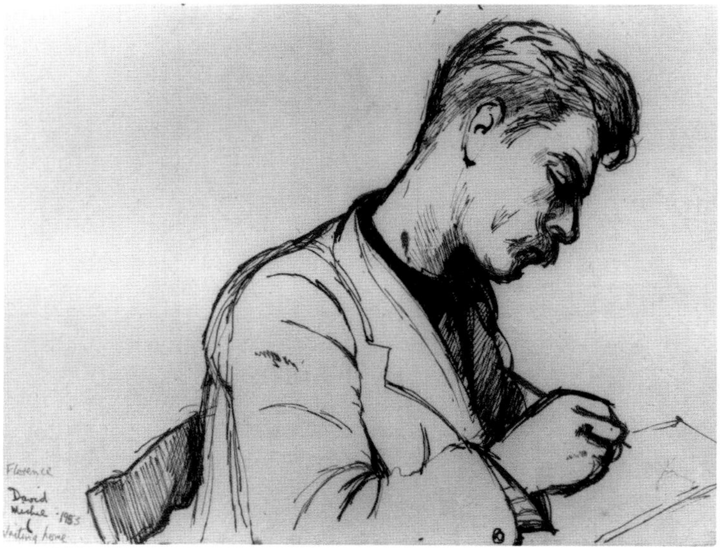

American painters in the series. In addition, we were getting magazines like *Picture Post*, which was important because it had very good photographs and articles on painters, usually from London. Because there was so little we swallowed up everything we could get hold of. Magazines started appearing from the Continent: *Domus* from Italy, which was mainly an architectural magazine but always featured contemporary Italian painters like Mario Sironi, who was painting industrial landscapes around Milan.

— *In the mid-1950s you went on a travelling scholarship to Italy with David Michie. Did your admiration for contemporary Italian art influence your decision to go there?*

I suppose it did. I was also keen on Giotto and Masaccio, the early Italian painters, and it seemed to be easier to get to Italy and travel there than in France at that time. We went to Paris and on to Italy, where students from Edinburgh had been going for years. When we arrived in Milan we saw a big exhibition from European art schools, including Edinburgh. We then hunted out private art galleries, who would look out works for us to see by Sironi, Morandi and others of interest. The Italians were much quicker at producing books on contemporary art and I managed to pick up one or two early on in Italy, which I still have. I think Sironi was the first one.

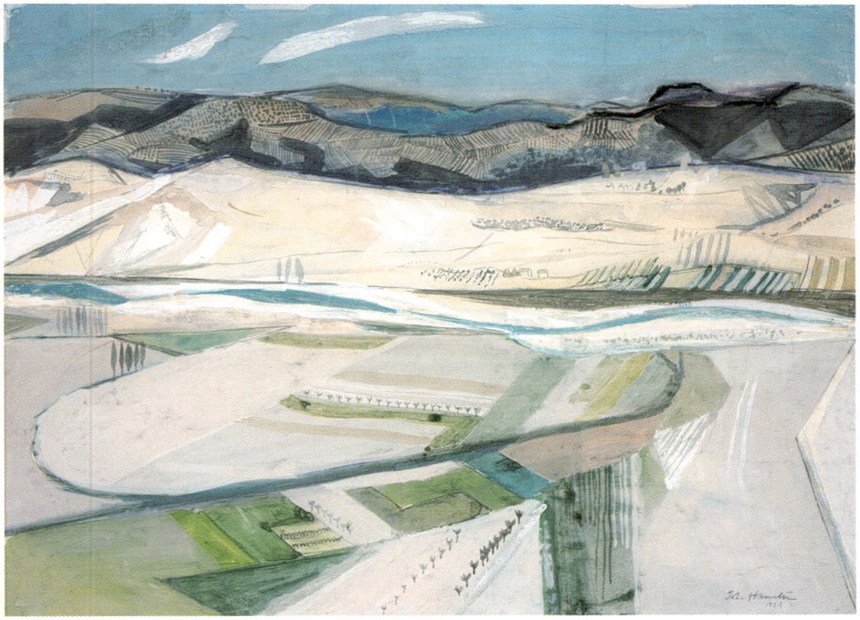

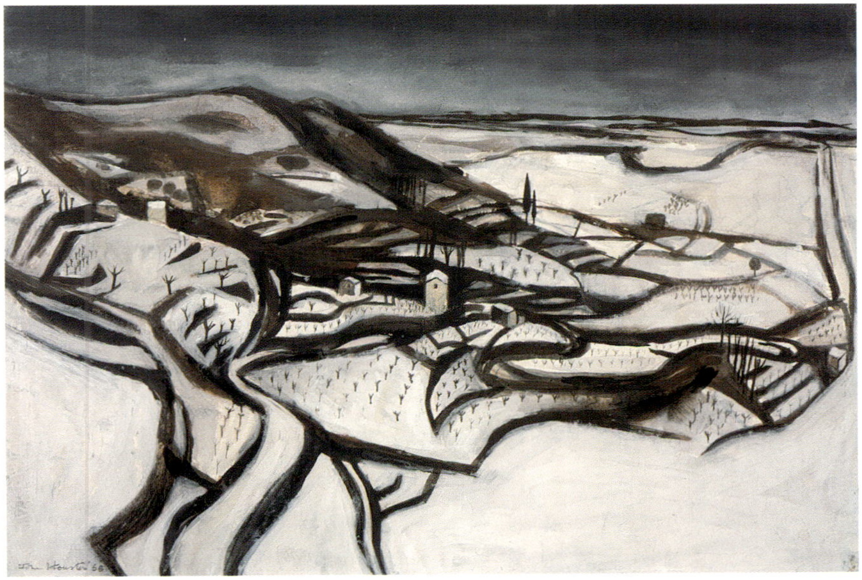

above: The Tiber Valley, Orvieto, 1954
Artist's collection · no.16

below: Winter, Anticoli, 1954
Artist's collection · no.19

— *In Italy, you seemed to be drawn to rural places to carry out your work, rather than the obvious artistic centres of Florence or Rome.*

David Michie and I stayed in Florence for six weeks as there was a lot we wanted to see and many of the artists we both liked. From there we went to Siena, where I found the art more decorative; I liked the rather severe style of the early Italian artists. Of course, we were also expected to do some work. When we began to paint outside, the landscape was really quite pretty; it was the beginning of October and everything was still green. It wasn't until Siena, when the time of year made the landscape appear stark, that it became more interesting for me.

— *There is a strong sense of the structure of the landscape in your Italian drawings and paintings. Seeing that countryside in those winter conditions seems to have allowed you to develop your art?*

Yes, I could see things to do with it, and it also related to some of the artists I was interested in. The landscape was similar in appearance to things they were doing. I remember I was very taken with the predella paintings of Fra Angelico, which set biblical scenes in a distinct type of landscape. Around Siena, the landscape was exactly like that, and so this was an expression of ideas about painting with which I was sympathetic.

— *Your Italian paintings do appear to be important to the future development of your work.* Village under the Cliffs, *from 1962, is richly coloured and painted, but it has an underlying structure of a similar tough quality.*

Yes, I suppose this can be traced back to my first year as a student under Henderson Blyth and his concern for the drawing and structure of a painting. That remained deeply embedded in me, alongside my interest in early and contemporary Italian artists.

— *Did you have a sense at that point, after you had produced those paintings in Italy, that your art was beginning to develop significantly?*

I was beginning to feel, I suppose, that a bit of it was mine. *Village under the Cliffs* had come about because Elizabeth, my wife, was given a commission by the Post Office to go to a village called Staithes, on the Yorkshire coast, to make a lithograph. There were artists all over Britain doing the same, producing images for a campaign to promote correct addresses on letters. This shows the next village down from Staithes, where we did quite a few drawings. When I came back I started this picture, and it's one of the first where I felt something different was coming about. The structure was still there, but it was less obvious. I was also becoming more interested in the actual picture-making process and the use of oil paint, as a lot of my earlier works were in gouache.

— *At that time, around 1960, you also made a series of works which show images of birds in a softer landscape than appears in either the paintings you made in Italy or in* Village under the Cliffs.

I had painted a few bird pictures in my third year as a student. I used to keep pigeons when I was a boy and drew quite a few of them. The miners in Fife were great pigeon fanciers and every weekend the railway station was full of baskets of pigeons, which were sent away to various destinations, sometimes in Scotland, sometimes in England, and as far away as France. I got my birds from the miners. They would give me one or two, and eventually I had twenty or thirty. I had started painting cornfields and bird shapes in the latter part of the 1950s, when we used to visit Henderson Blyth, who had gone to teach at Aberdeen. At the

opposite: Village under the Cliffs, 1962
Scottish National Gallery of Modern Art, Edinburgh · no.24

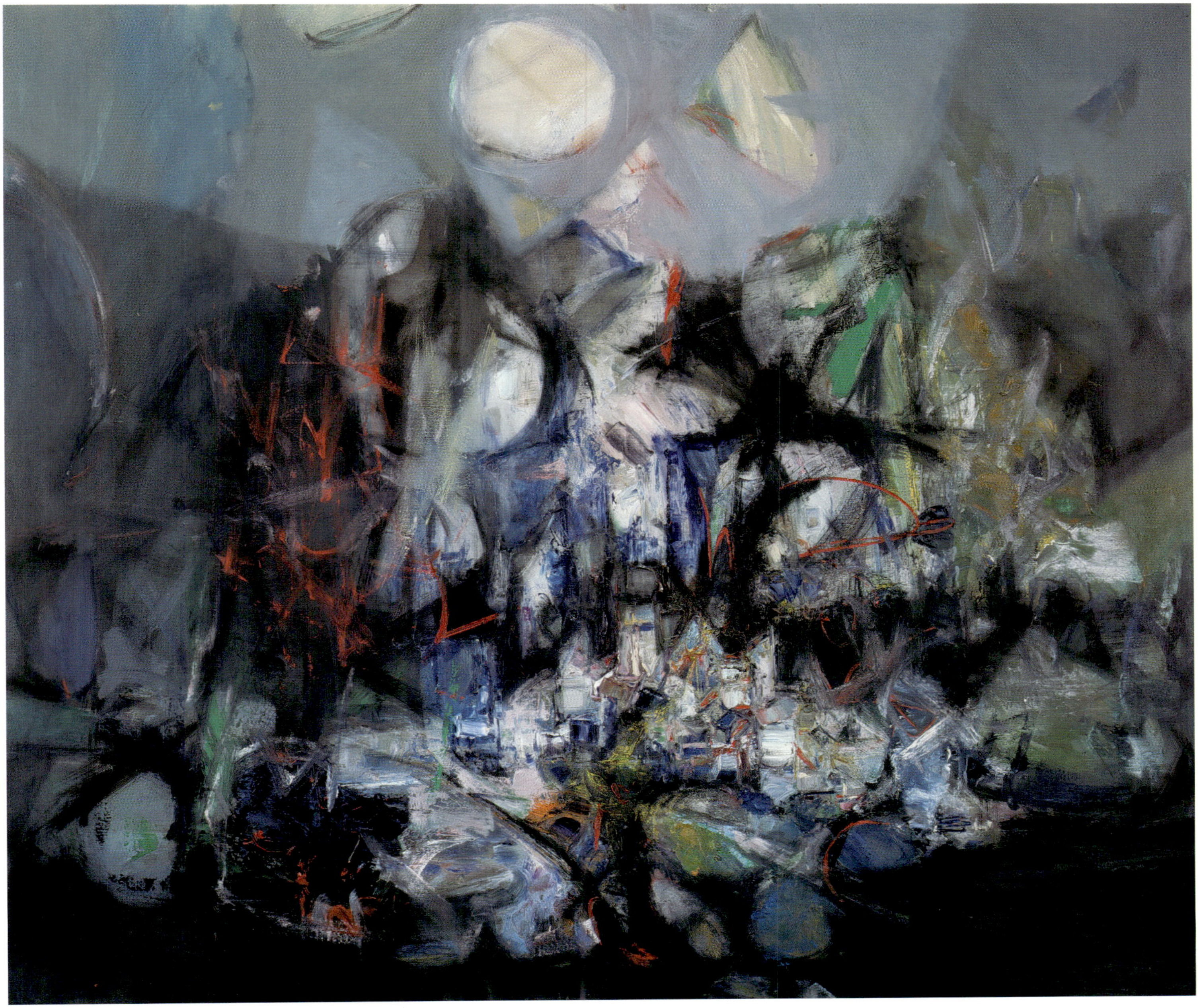

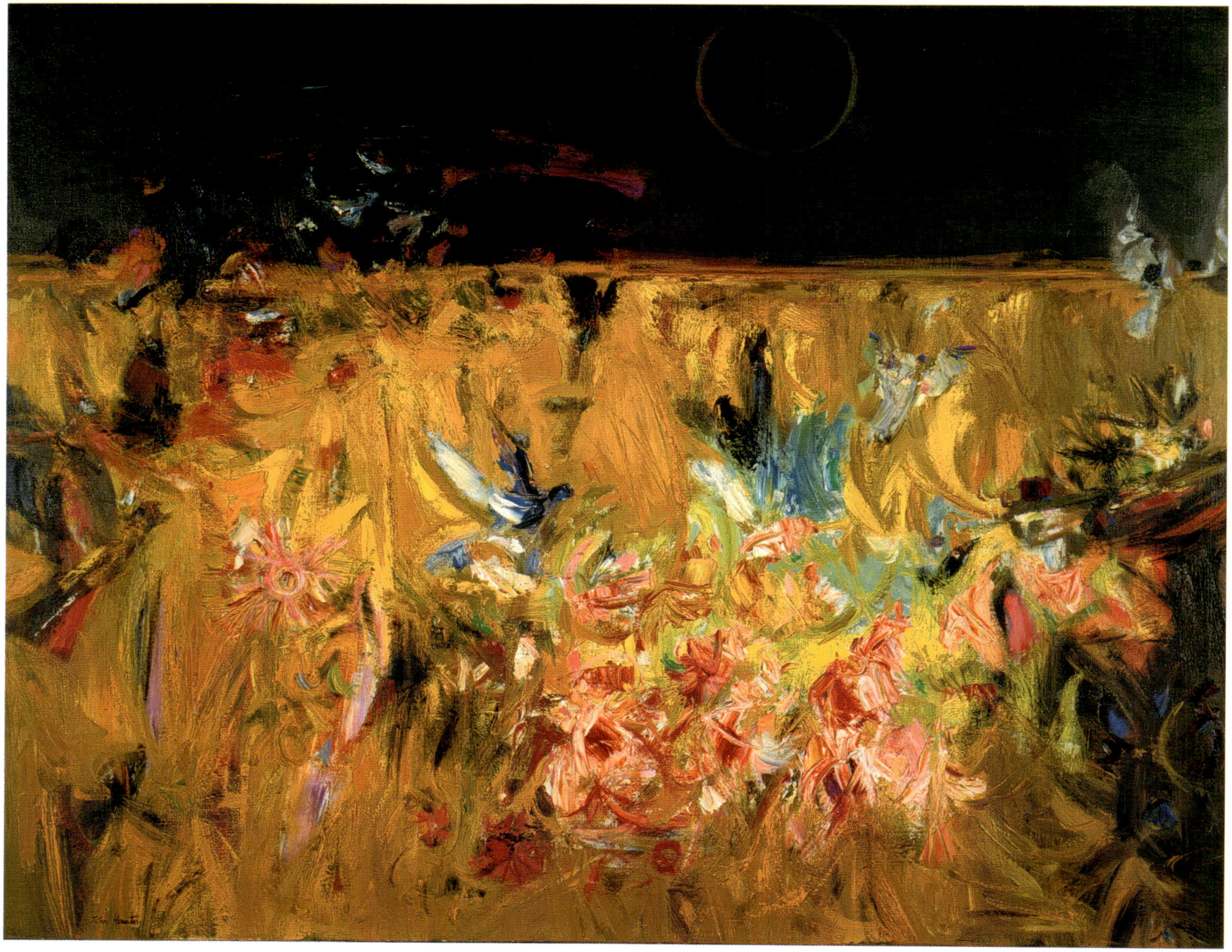

Birds, Flowers and Dark Sun, *c.*1962

Scottish National Gallery of Modern Art, Edinburgh · no.23

same time, my watercolour painting started showing certain ways I might develop oil painting. I had been doing a series of large watercolours in the late 1950s and the freer use of the paint, where one colour bled into another, suggested ways I might use oil paint. Of course, the gentle landscape of Aberdeenshire was very different from the blocky, fort-like Italian villages, where everything was cubistic and spartan. I was going back to my own landscape, which I had never really looked at. I hadn't done much landscape painting, as I had painted mainly industrial subjects. I'm glad now I painted these pictures of cornfields and hedgerows, as many of them have now gone.

— *Can I ask you about a major event in your life in the 1950s, your meeting with Elizabeth Blackadder, whom you subsequently married. You have both become successful painters. Would you say this process has been competitive at any time?*

No, not at all. I didn't meet Elizabeth at the start of college as she was a year below me and, because I played football every Saturday and went home every Friday night, I missed a lot of the socialising in my first four years. I would arrive on a Monday morning, stay with my aunt, paint, go to the cinema, do my football training at the Hearts ground at Tynecastle, and then go home on a Friday night. But I was also very keen on dancing, and the college had a great dance every two weeks; it was there, in my postgraduate year in 1952–3 that I met Elizabeth. I had known her by sight, but I had not talked to her. We both seemed to like many of the same things so there was no barrier. In retrospect, my painting then was almost like hers is now, rather severe I suppose, while she was a much freer painter of landscapes and flowers. In some ways we've almost reversed roles over the years. We never fell out or said, 'What on earth are you painting that for?' or, 'Why are you interested in these painters?' She was also studying art history at Edinburgh University and, through Professor Talbot Rice, was interested in Byzantine art. She took me to

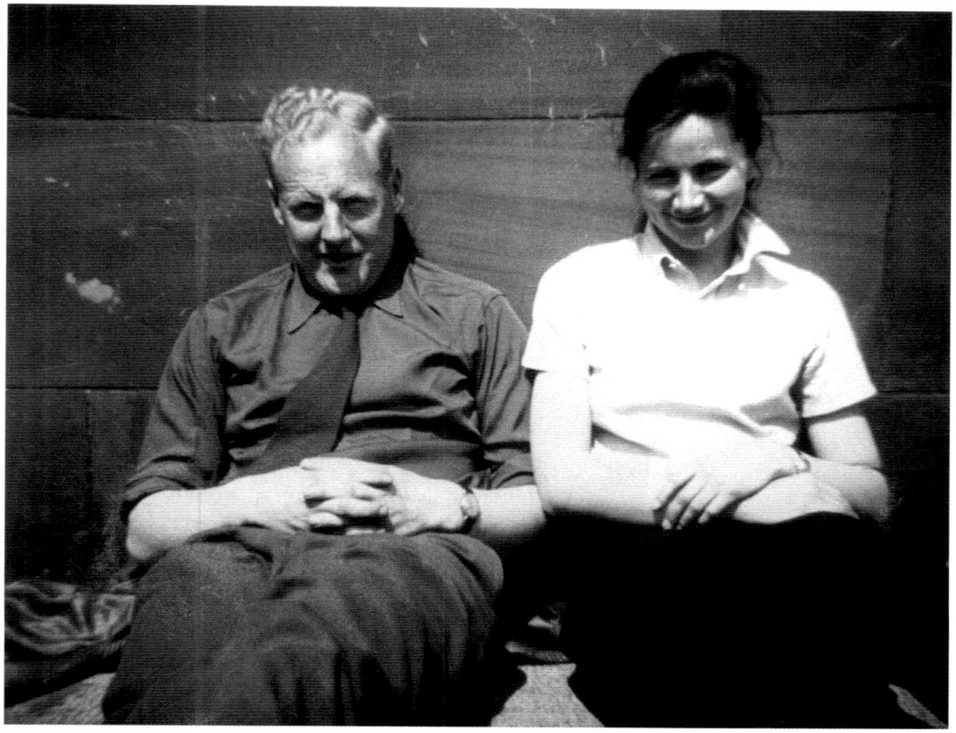

John Houston and Elizabeth Blackadder, 1953
Artist's collection

Yugoslavia and Greece to see Byzantine painting, and I introduced her to my kind of painting in Italy, and also to some of the other things I liked. I don't think she had ever been to a western film in her life! Her mother didn't approve of that! It was alright to go and see Laurence Olivier in *Henry V*, but not western or gangster films! We both helped to draw each other out. I introduced Elizabeth to jazz and she introduced me to some of her favourite music: Schubert, Mozart, Schumann. I had quite a successful first exhibition, so we were able to buy a car and we went to France. We travelled all over Normandy and Brittany, as we wanted to see churches and stained glass. We visited Chartres and another time went to see the Romanesque painting in the churches south of the Loire, which I didn't know anything about, but which Elizabeth did.

— *You taught at Edinburgh College of Art for many years, from 1955 to 1989, which is in itself an impressive commitment, but there is also your prodigious career as an exhibiting artist. How did you manage this amount of work?*

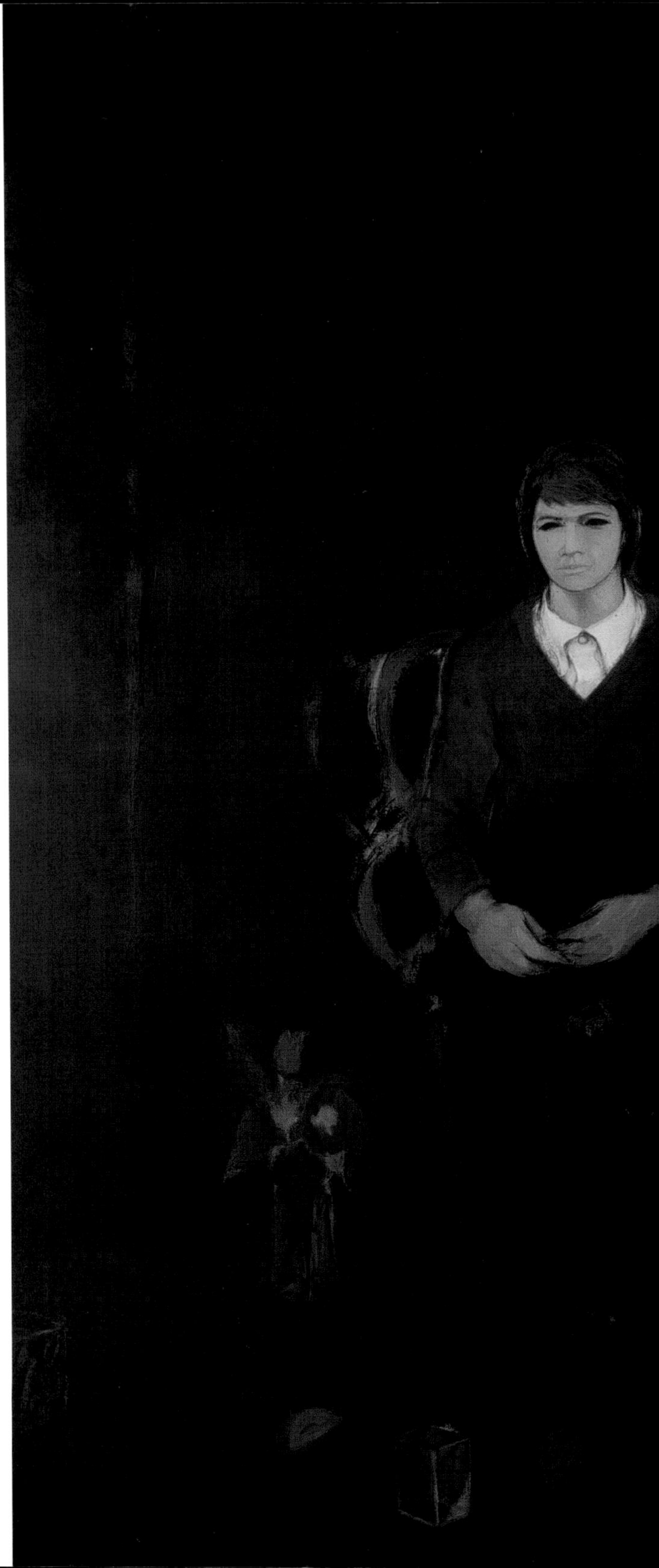

Elizabeth and Cat, 1977

Artist's collection · no.33

Well, I took early retirement in 1989! I don't know how I found time to go to college four days a week and still paint. Gillies was strict, in that it didn't matter if you had an exhibition coming up, you were still expected to be there at 9.30am and teach through the day and into the evening.

I used to meet people from Glasgow or the Royal College of Art in London who would say: 'we're not going in for the next two or three weeks because we've got an exhibition coming up.' I would reply: 'You wouldn't last five minutes in Edinburgh!'

I used to discuss this with David McClure and David Michie, as I wondered how they did any work because of their different lives. David thought it would be difficult to be married to another artist. But as Elizabeth and I were both painters, we found we were able to work away constantly. Many of my contemporaries showed a lot of promise but for various reasons, often personal, the discipline of working fell away and they just disappeared. I feel extremely lucky to be married to an equally committed painter like Elizabeth.

— *Did you ever feel a wish to move elsewhere?*

I was asked to go to Aberdeen, but when the principal and head of department at Edinburgh heard about this they made me a better offer. Henderson Blyth knew that if I was on the staff, he would also get Elizabeth as a possible part-time teacher. Some of the students I had met at the Rome School in Italy had begun teaching in London, but they had the same kind of life as we had, so there seemed to be no reason to go there. At that time there were very few places showing young artists. The generation of Henry Moore, Graham Sutherland and Matthew Smith was showing in the galleries.

— *So, by comparison, you felt that it was possible to make a good career in Scotland?*

We never thought of a career at that time. We were just working – though we were never well paid – and then only for the hours we taught. For the three months in the summer we didn't get anything, and we were not paid when we were ill. With the two of us teaching we managed, but there was nowhere to exhibit except the big societies, in particular the Society of Scottish Artists, which was where our age group was showing. In 1959 William Macaulay, who had been deputy director at Kelvingrove [Glasgow Art Gallery], became a partner in Aitken Dott's in Castle Street, Edinburgh. Elizabeth had worked at Kelvingrove for two summers, helping to catalogue the collection, and had got to know him, which is how my connection with Aitken Dott started. In that first year they sold some of my works, then a collector came up from London, a Mrs Oliver Parker, who had a very good collection of Nicolas de Staël, Chaïm Soutine and British artists, and she bought a few. I had my first exhibition at the gallery in 1960, which was very successful. Before that in 1957, a group of us had founded the 57 Gallery, which was a sheer bit of luck. It was a second floor studio in George Street belonging to Daphne Dyce-Sharp, who was a sculptor. She was getting married and moving to Canada, but she had paid the rent for a year or two, and said, 'Why don't you use it as a gallery?' There was enough space for about twelve pictures, and a rack for portfolios. Nobody ran it. When it was my turn I put my pictures up, set out my portfolio, and sat there myself. I sold a few things!

— *The work* Bathers, *which dates from the mid-1960s, might be said to be unusual in your work, because of the presence of figures. Figures occur again in other paintings, like the much later* Three Painters by the Sea, *but the subject of landscape dominates your painting.*

Well, *Bathers* is only one of a few figure paintings I completed at that time. They developed after I had been painting landscapes in a fairly free way, and I began to feel that I didn't want to repeat that subject matter and I also had a desire for a simpler, stricter composition. Also, I had become interested in artists like Francis Bacon and Willem de Kooning. I had always drawn a lot from the model when I was teaching; I taught anatomy for fourteen years. (I even managed to get John Bellany to do some anatomy drawing, which was something!) With Bacon and de Kooning it was interesting to see what contemporary painters were doing with the figure, because a lot of painting up to that time, especially painting in France – Nicolas de Staël, Alfred Manessier and others – had been very abstract. I was never an abstract painter in that respect. I always felt I needed a connection with subject matter; then, suddenly, here were two or three very interesting artists working with the figure – Richard Diebenkorn was another, as well as Pierre Bonnard, whom I always admired.

— *By the end of that decade, however, a phase began in your painting when it was at its most abstract. This seems to have*

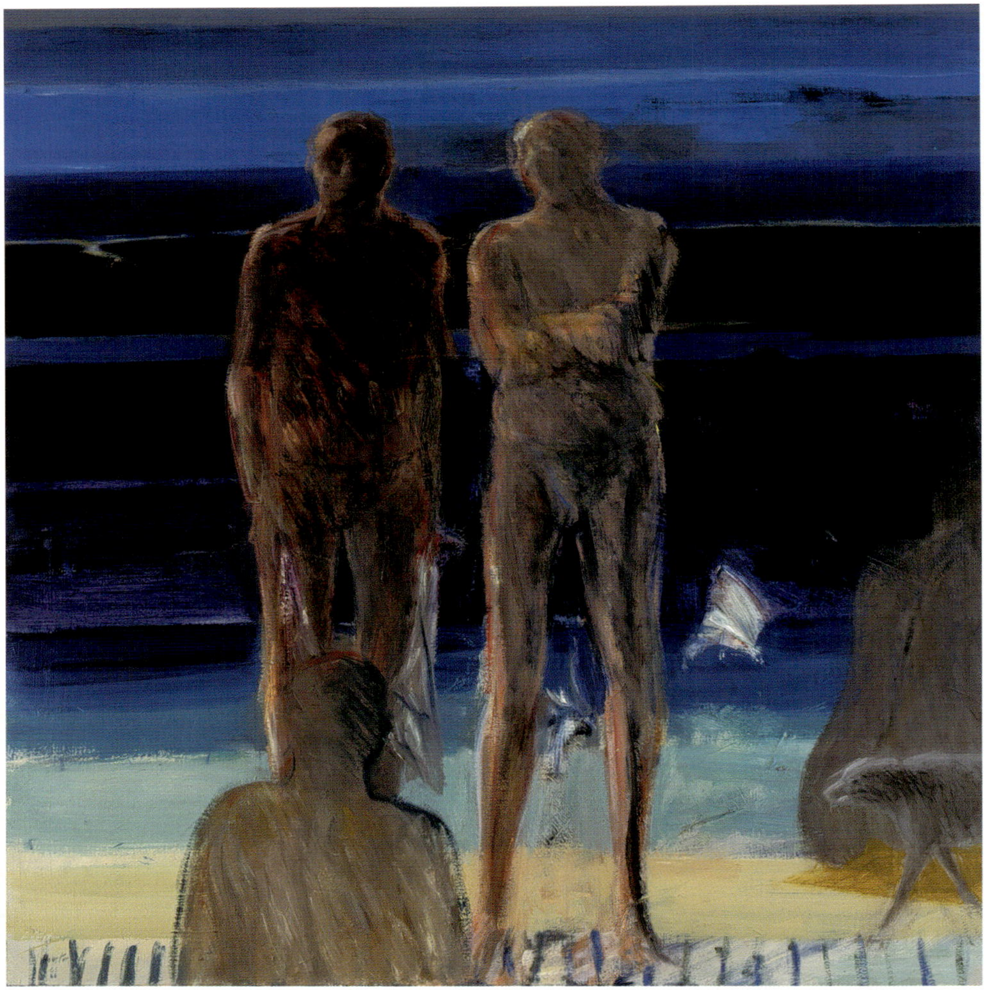

Bathers, 1965–6
Scottish National Gallery of Modern Art, Edinburgh · no.26

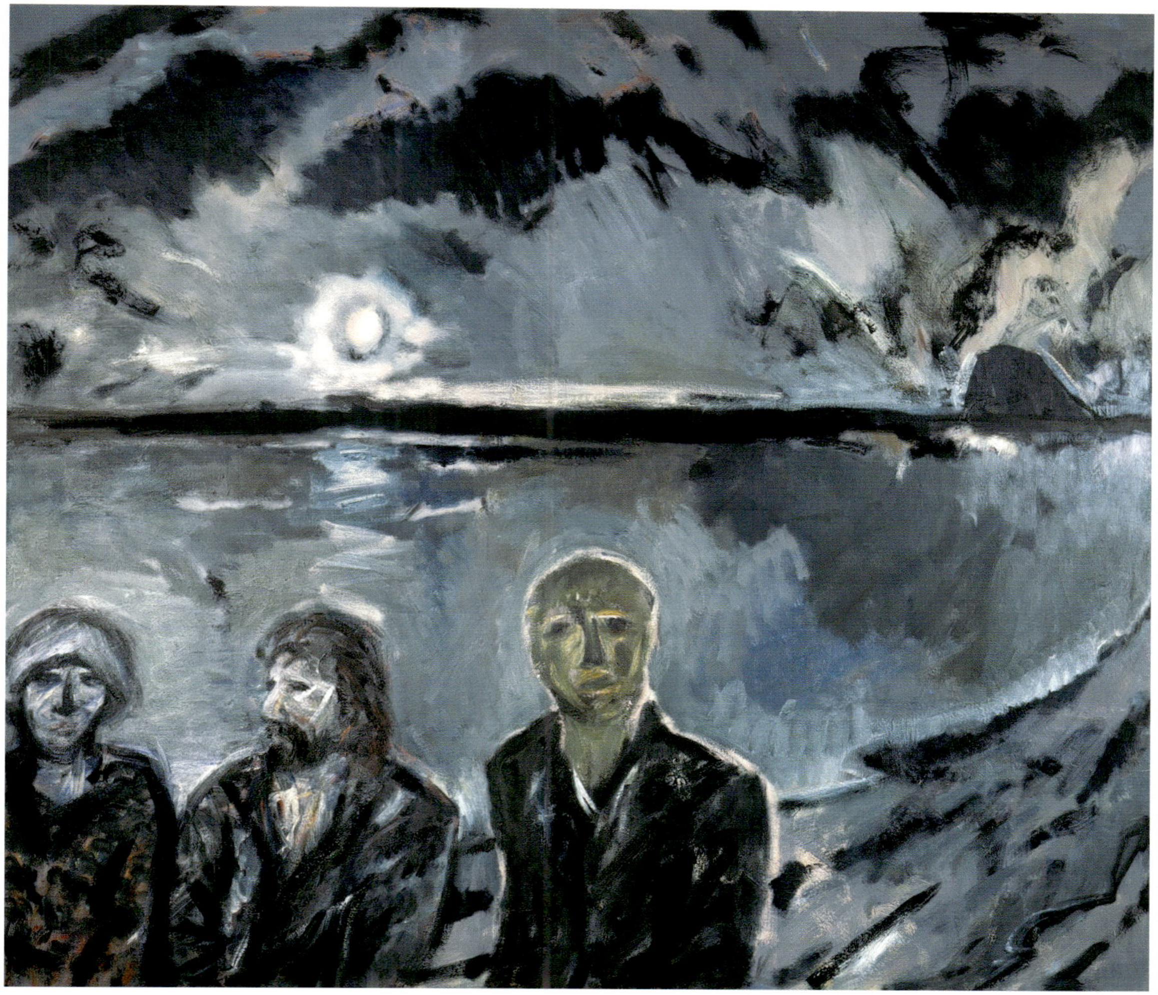

Three Painters by the Sea (Elizabeth Blackadder, John Bellany, John Houston), 1984

Artist's collection · no.36

happened after your visit to the United States in 1969.

Yes, the most abstract it ever would be. The American trip came following an exhibition I had had in 1962. I received a letter from a Mrs Johnson in London, saying she had seen one of my pictures and that she would like to visit me. She bought four works which were sent out to America. It was only then that I realised who she was. Her husband, Sam, was the only son of S. C. Johnson of Johnson Wax, and they were travelling around the world visiting all the various companies they ran. They wanted me to go to Wisconsin to paint the fall landscape and they also asked, 'Could I bring an exhibition with me?' We stayed in New York with a few days to look around, and then went up to Racine in Wisconsin. They admired British education, so they had built a school there for their four children and then invited another 350 children to become pupils! They had quite a few British teachers and all the children had navy-blue blazers and grey flannels – girls and boys! I was the artist-in-residence at the school, near the Johnson Foundation which was in a large Frank Lloyd Wright house named Wingspread that had been the Johnson family home. They had stayed in it but it had been very difficult to live in. Racine was a small city of about 100,000 people and was the headquarters of Johnson Wax. We did a little painting there, but the place we were destined for was Lake Owen in north Wisconsin, about sixty miles south of Lake Superior. Eventually, we got a phone call saying the colours were turning. We were picked up and taken to their airport; this huge hanger with a polished parquet floor, jets and helicopters parked on it. I said, 'that's a wonderful floor', and was astonished when they said, 'this is where we test all our polishes'. They wanted very big pictures, the biggest I had ever painted, about nine by seven feet. The canvases were rolled and taken up the gangway of the plane. We were at Lake Owen for about ten or twelve days and I painted around five works, which I haven't seen to this day. When I came back to Scotland, I carried on with the subject, as I had brought some sketches back. On the return journey we saw a wonderful exhibition in New York of American painting, beginning with Milton Avery and Edward Hopper and continuing to the present day, with a strong representation of work by Jasper Johns, de Kooning, Adolph Gottlieb and Jackson Pollock.

— *Was that the first time you had seen work by these artists?*

We had seen some in New York on the way out, but had concentrated on Matisse and Picasso in the Museum of Modern Art and the Guggenheim Collection. This was the first time we had seen such a collection and it was extremely impressive. That, and the very difficult landscape at Wisconsin, certainly made me think about things. At Wisconsin it wasn't possible to see anything unless you were at the edge of a lake or on a road, because everything was so flat and full of trees. That was when I started painting sky pictures, because I was very conscious of the low horizon and this huge sky. This gave me a structure, which was influenced by those American painters. It was to do with an atmospheric use of paint but, underlying it, something very simple like the horizontal or the vertical or the curve, like the curve of the sky or of the clouds. I felt the paintings were just going to be loose bits of painting and would collapse unless I had that structure. I saw that this was something that de Kooning had achieved. And, as well as being keen on

Stormy Sunset over the Sea, *c.*1972
Royal Bank of Scotland Group Collection · no.29

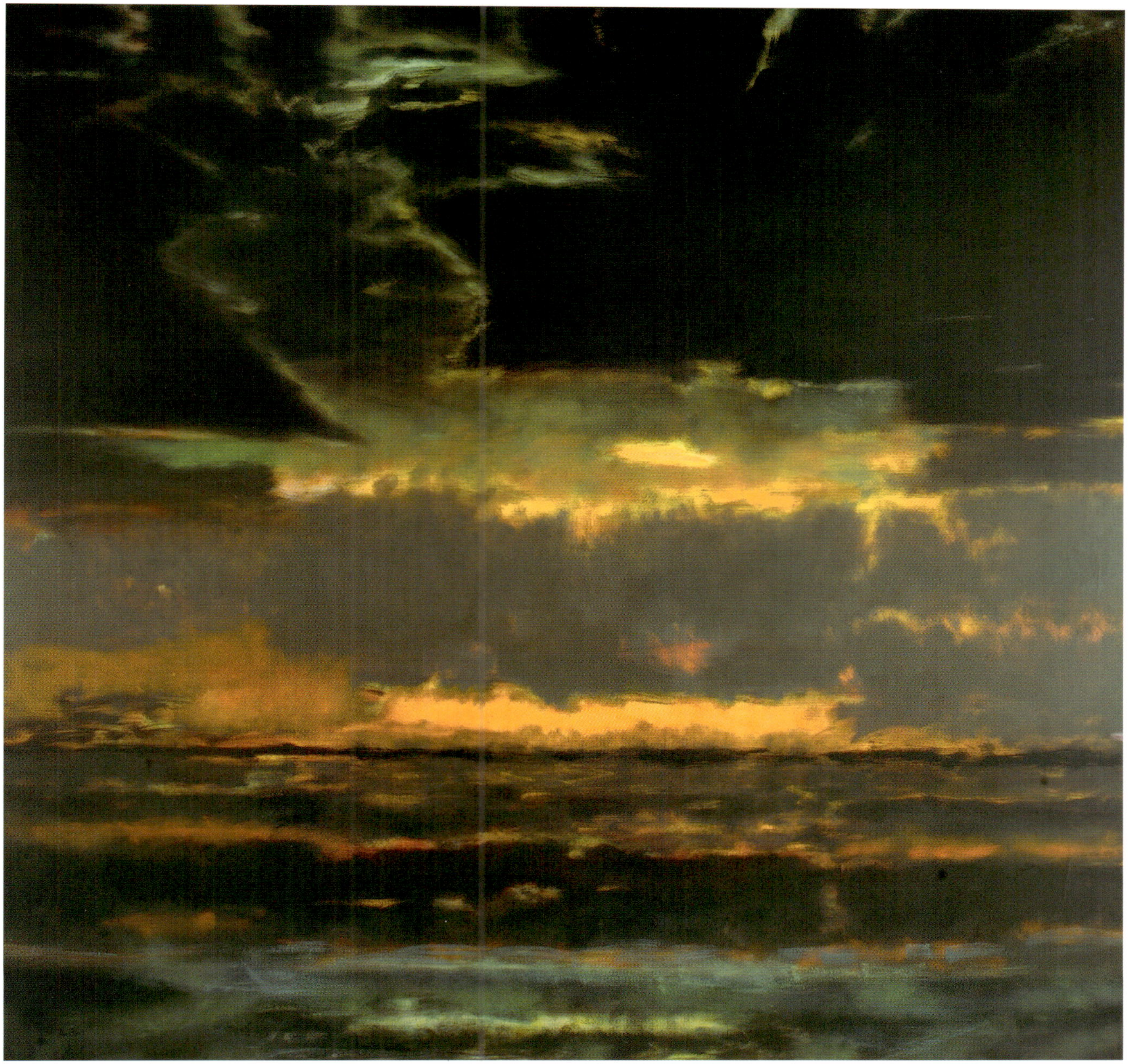

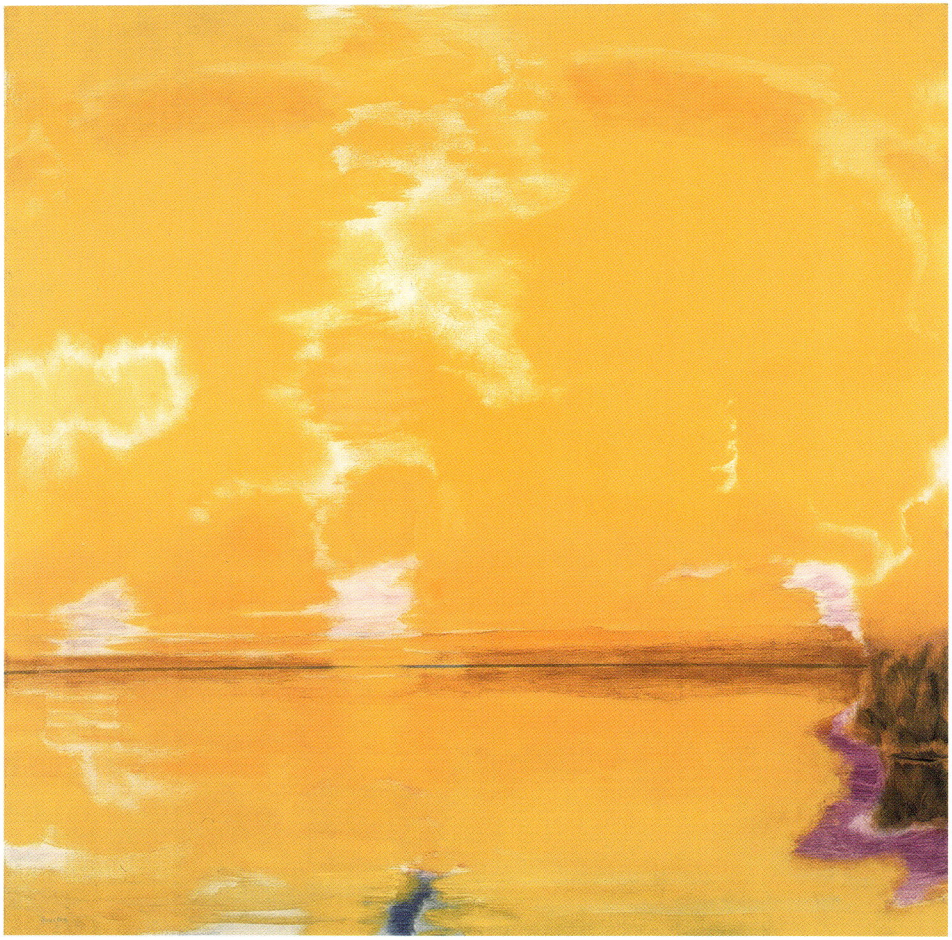

above: Golden Lake II, 1971
Artist's collection · no.27

opposite: Cliffs, Les Petites-Dalles, 1978–80
Artist's collection · no.34

some of those American painters, I had also been doing a lot of large watercolours on Japanese paper in which the colour bled away. That softness combined with this structure suggested a way of working.

— *This seems to relate back to the development of your work in the 1950s, and the ongoing importance of an underlying structure as a part of your compositions.*

Yes, people never think of it, but I'm aware of that in nearly every painting I do.

— *In the late 1970s a new phase appears in your work, which is well expressed in a painting such as* Cliffs, Les Petites-Dalles. *It has the same concern with the effect of paint on canvas, but it is less of an independent abstract statement than works such as* Golden Lake II *from the beginning of that decade. What were the circumstances which brought about this change?*

After our return from America I worked on a number of paintings based on that experience, like *Golden Lake II*. We realised we had never been to the north of Scotland, so we went to Caithness and then Harris, two years running, and made a lot of watercolours there. Then, suddenly, I felt I had done that and, for the first time ever, I didn't know where the next body of work

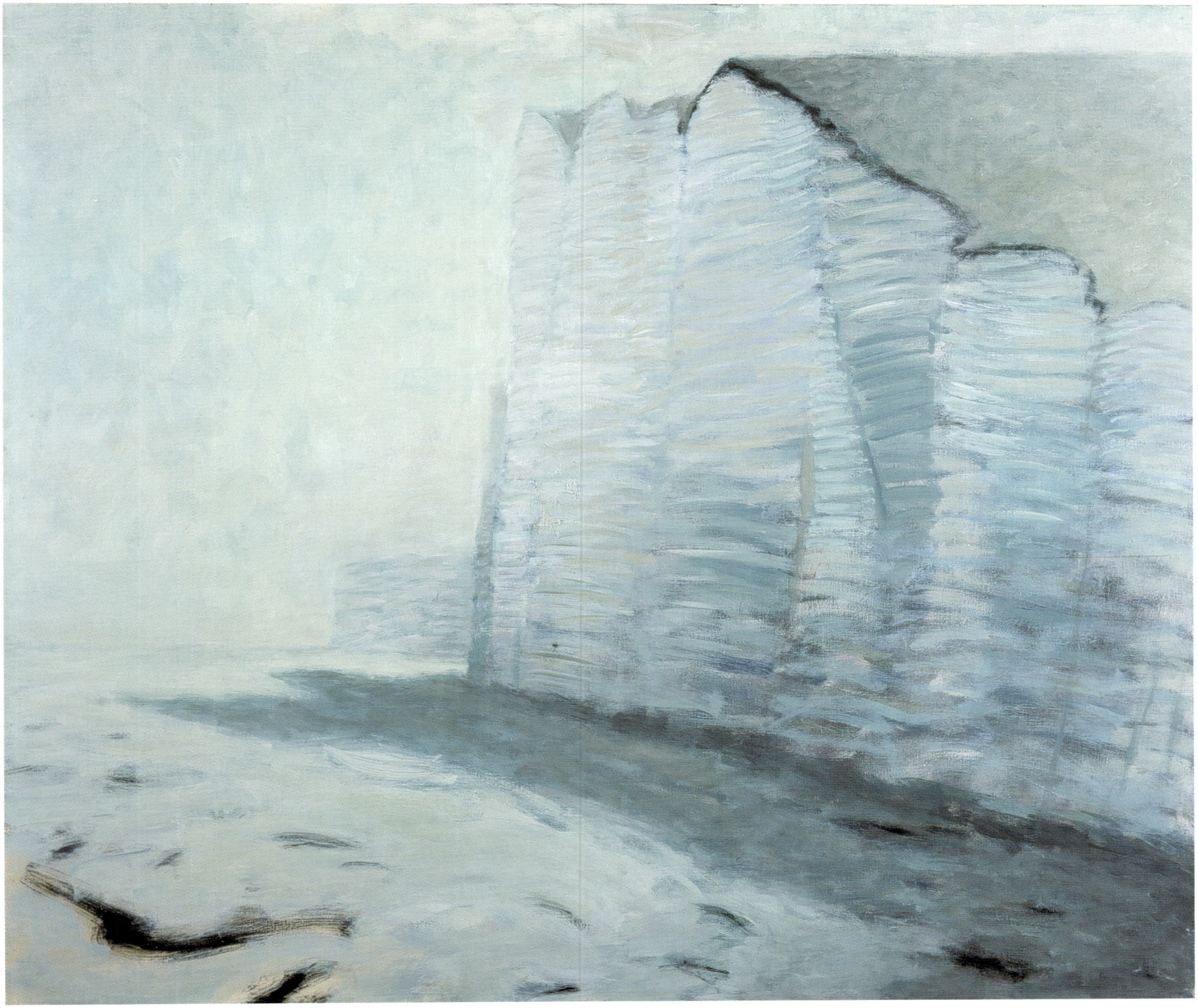

was going to come from. I tried various things, a lot of which I destroyed and I had two or three not very productive years. It was also a time, similar to the last year or two, when the question was being asked, 'is painting finished?' Conceptual art was beginning to appear and I really couldn't grip this at all. The artists I admired throughout history had always produced an object, whether it was a painting, sculpture or a building. Conceptualism threw me and came at a time when I had my own worries about repetition in my work.

— *Were you conscious of the continuing efforts being made by other British figurative painters at the time, who were being overshadowed by conceptual work?*

Not only them but many of the American painters; they were all in the same boat. Later I realised they were often having the same problems as I was. My friends here were dealing with the same issues, finding it very difficult to come to terms with such a break, where no object was being produced. At Documenta in Kassel or at the Venice Biennale we would walk into rooms with slide projectors or just a series of photographs on display, and it was extremely difficult to think how we fitted into this. This was additionally problematic because of difficulties I was having anyway, questioning where I could go with my paintings of Harris at night, which were mostly dark grey on black.

— *The Harris works must be the most reductive paintings you have done, sometimes just washes of very dark colour.*

Yes, I thought of them, 'Well there's not much I can do to simplify this any more!' But then we went back to Brittany and Normandy and I became interested in Monet's late paintings of tree trunks and grasses. We visited the places he painted, for example, Petites-Dalles, which is why that work came about. We both did a lot of drawings of that particular part of the coast. It gave me a new subject, but also a structure or a subject to hang on to, and with this a confidence that painting wasn't finished.

— *Can we talk about what seems to be a particularly ambitious period in your career, from the early 1980s onwards, when you made a succession of landscape paintings mostly of the East Lothian coast, which are not only large in scale but newly experimental in their range of expression, colour and pattern.*

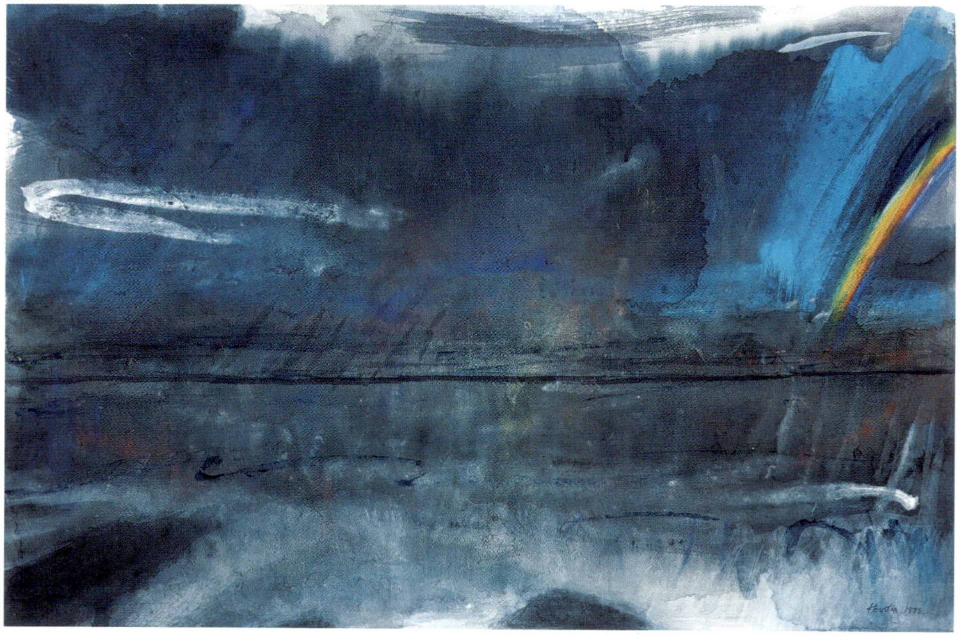

above: Night Sky, Harris I, 1975

Artist's collection · no.31

opposite: Rainbow over the Sea, Harris, 1975

Elizabeth Blackadder · no.32

Well, in addition to trips made to France, we visited southern Germany, and I was interested in Kandinsky and other painters in Germany from that time. I had come out of that difficult period in the 1970s and was more confident, full of ideas and energy. I was beginning to work on a large scale again, which I felt I needed for the subjects and sense of space I wanted to create. I was busy teaching and painting and things were going well after that bad time. I was still self-critical, but at least I wasn't worrying and thinking, 'What on earth am I painting pictures for?'

— *In 1986 you visited Japan for the first time. That experience seems to have brought about a new graphic quality in your compositions, stylistically setting them apart from the more traditionally expressionist handling of your earlier works.*

I made no paintings or drawings at all on that first trip. I had seen things that I liked in artworks and Japanese screens, but I hadn't been all that interested in the landscape there. When we went back the following year I became interested in oriental scroll paintings and ink drawings, and the work *Kyoto* came from that experience. I was beginning to see a connection between these Japanese paintings and the early landscape paintings of Picasso and Braque, and early Kandinsky. I jump backwards and forwards between various people I like, though Munch has probably been the greatest influence.

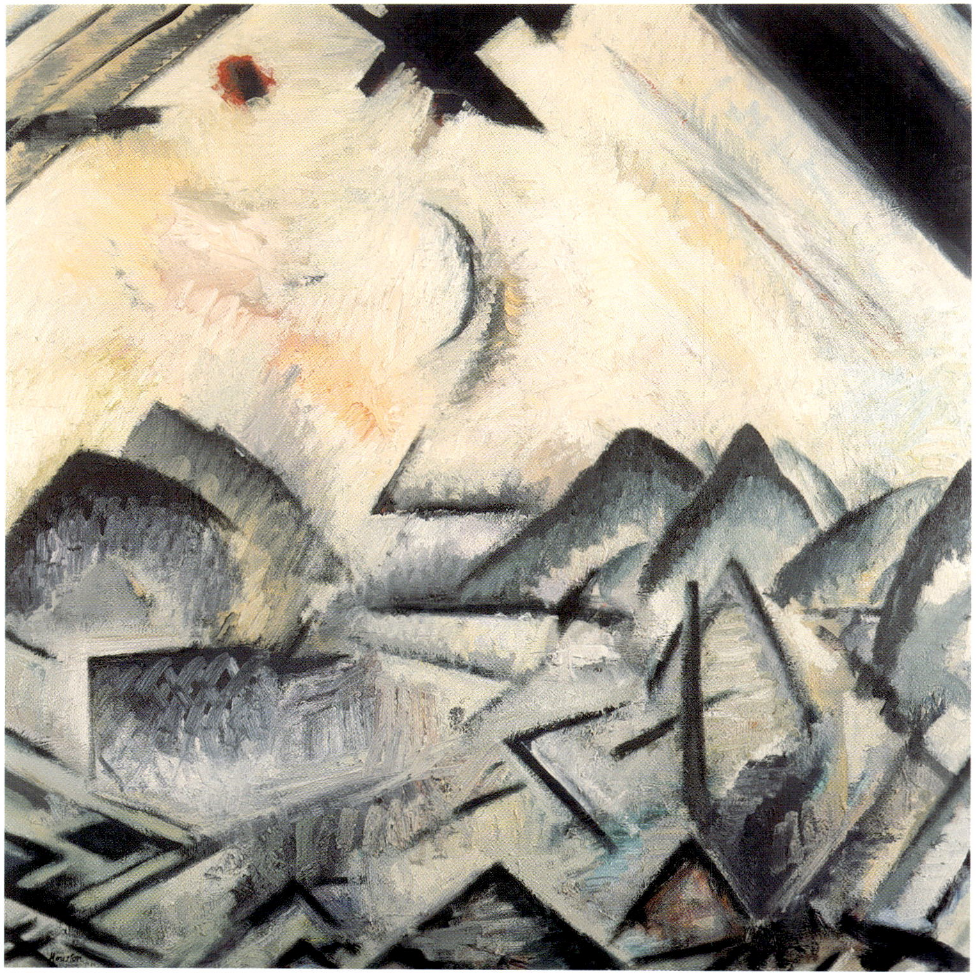

Kyoto, 1987
Artist's collection · no.39

— *Do you ever have in mind existing images, images of other paintings, when you are painting?*

Munch's work would make me look again at things around me – the sea, sky, and the rocks. Some of those Bass Rock scenes developed out of Munch's Norwegian paintings of winter or forests or of starry nights. They gave me a lead. But from early on, as with the industrial subjects, I've been influenced primarily by things around me and places I have been to and know.

— *Could you tell me something about your working habits? Do you work every day?*

Pretty well. Even though we are both retired – I retired in 1989, Elizabeth two years before me – we have found it extremely difficult to break the habit of how we taught during the day and came back and painted in the evenings and throughout the weekends and holidays.

— *So what is a typical day?*

In the morning both of us deal with business: letters to be dealt with, photography to be done, frames to be ordered, shopping, materials to collect, washing brushes, scraping palettes – all the business of being a painter. We try to get all that done by midday. We both then like to look at what we have been working on the day before. I sit for an hour before lunch to see how things might go from there. After lunch we take a break and then from about 4pm start work, until 9pm. At the weekend we work much more steadily.

— *Other than when you are travelling, do you have long breaks from painting?*

We don't paint as much on our travels as we used to. We used to do a lot of watercolours, quite large ones, up until nine or

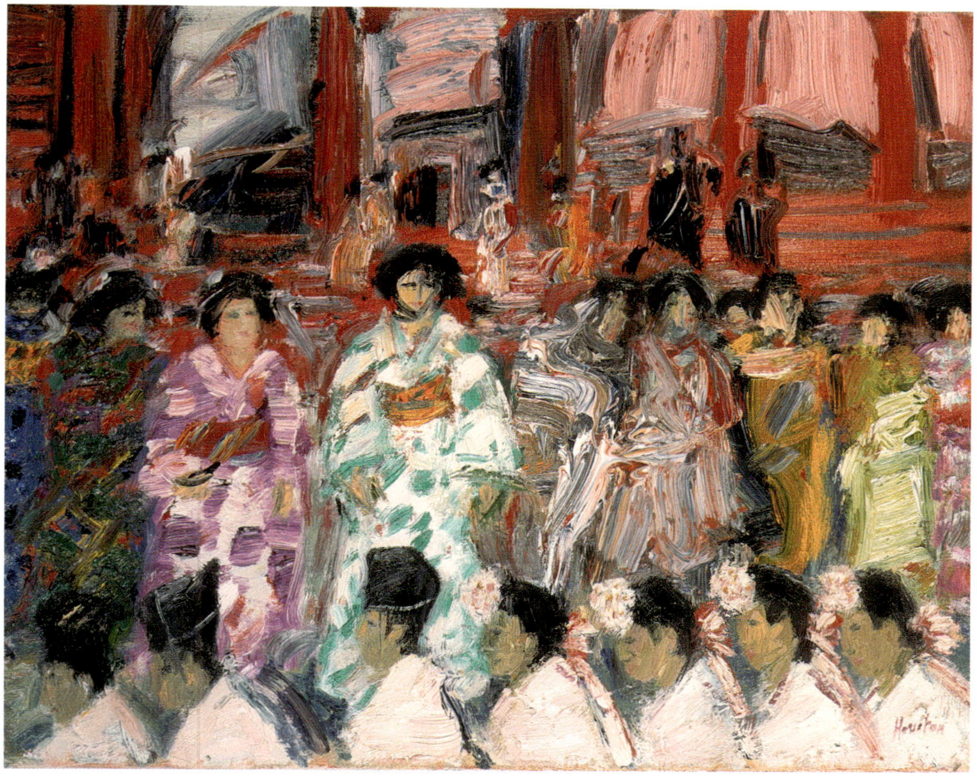

Shinto Festival, Kyoto, 1994–5
Private collection · no.48

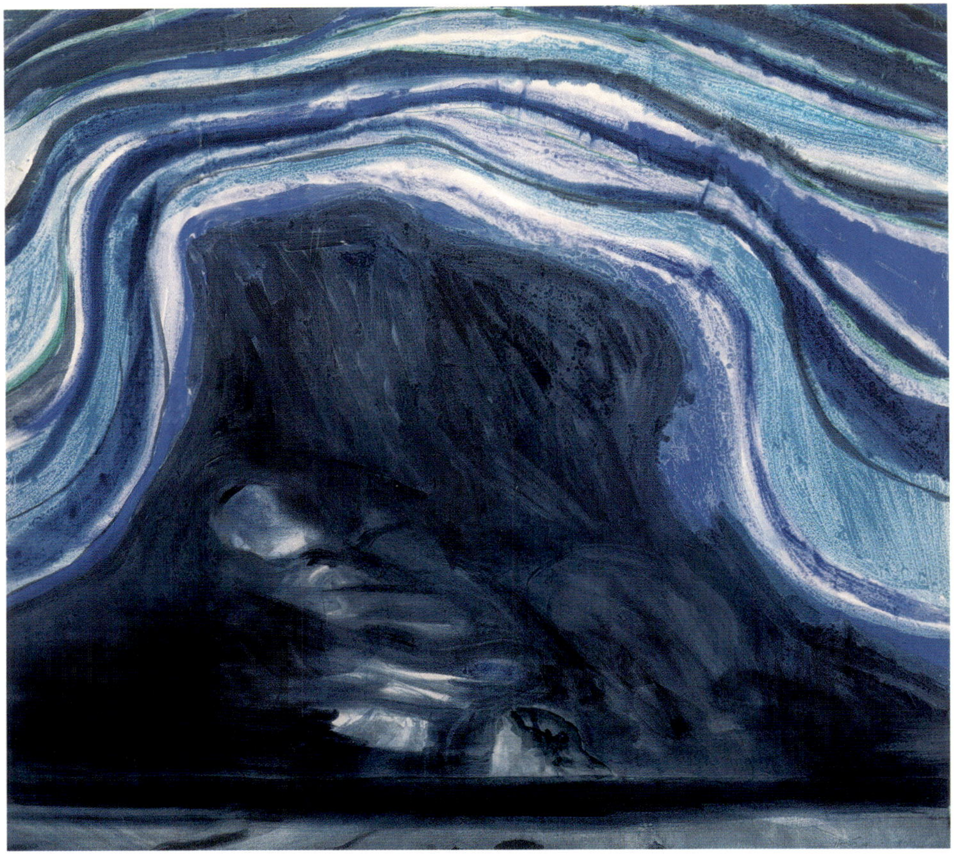

above: Evening Sky over the Bass Rock, 1964
Artist's collection · no.25

opposite: Low Tide, North Berwick, 1985
John Bellany · no.38

ten years ago, especially when we were going to Brittany. I did a lot of drawing. We drew and painted every day in these places. When we came back, some things never developed any further. Some of them later became paintings. It would be unusual to have a day in Edinburgh when I wouldn't do some work.

— *Your sketch books are full of studies of the landscape. How much of your work do you do outside?*

I have worked outside with oil paint, but it was such a performance. I would take an easel and some boards, paints, and that was fine when everything was dry. I would walk for half a mile or so from the car into the fields and paint, but it was always awkward taking it back – wet, dirty brushes and wet canvases, dust blowing on the painting – so after one or two goes I thought, 'that's that'. I thought about it once or twice again, about doing something much smaller and more easily manageable. We've both worked outside on quite a large scale in watercolour.

— *Apart from those practical disadvantages, is there a sense for you that working on paper in watercolour and the immediacy of that is something more appropriate for outside, and that oil is a better technique*

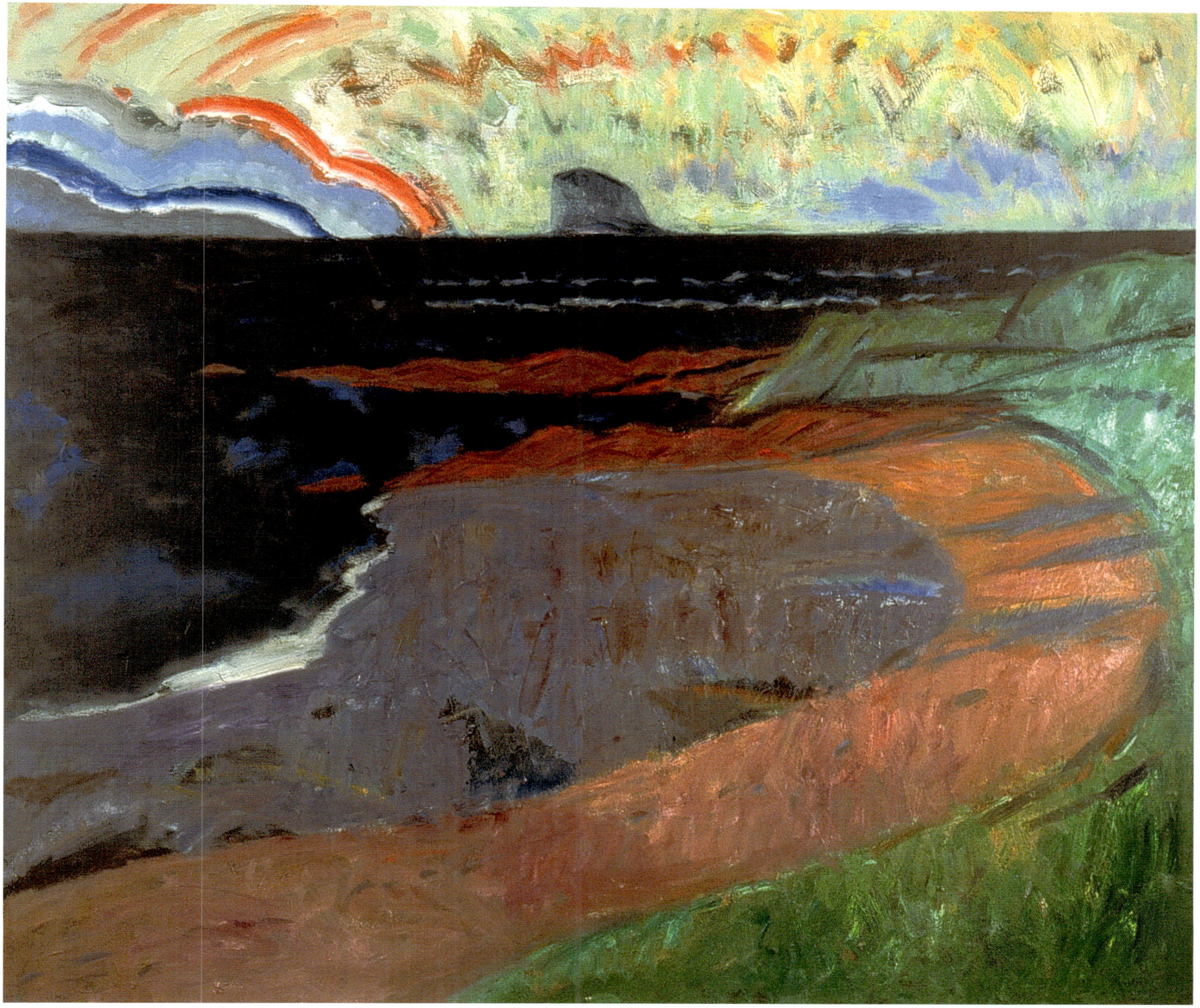

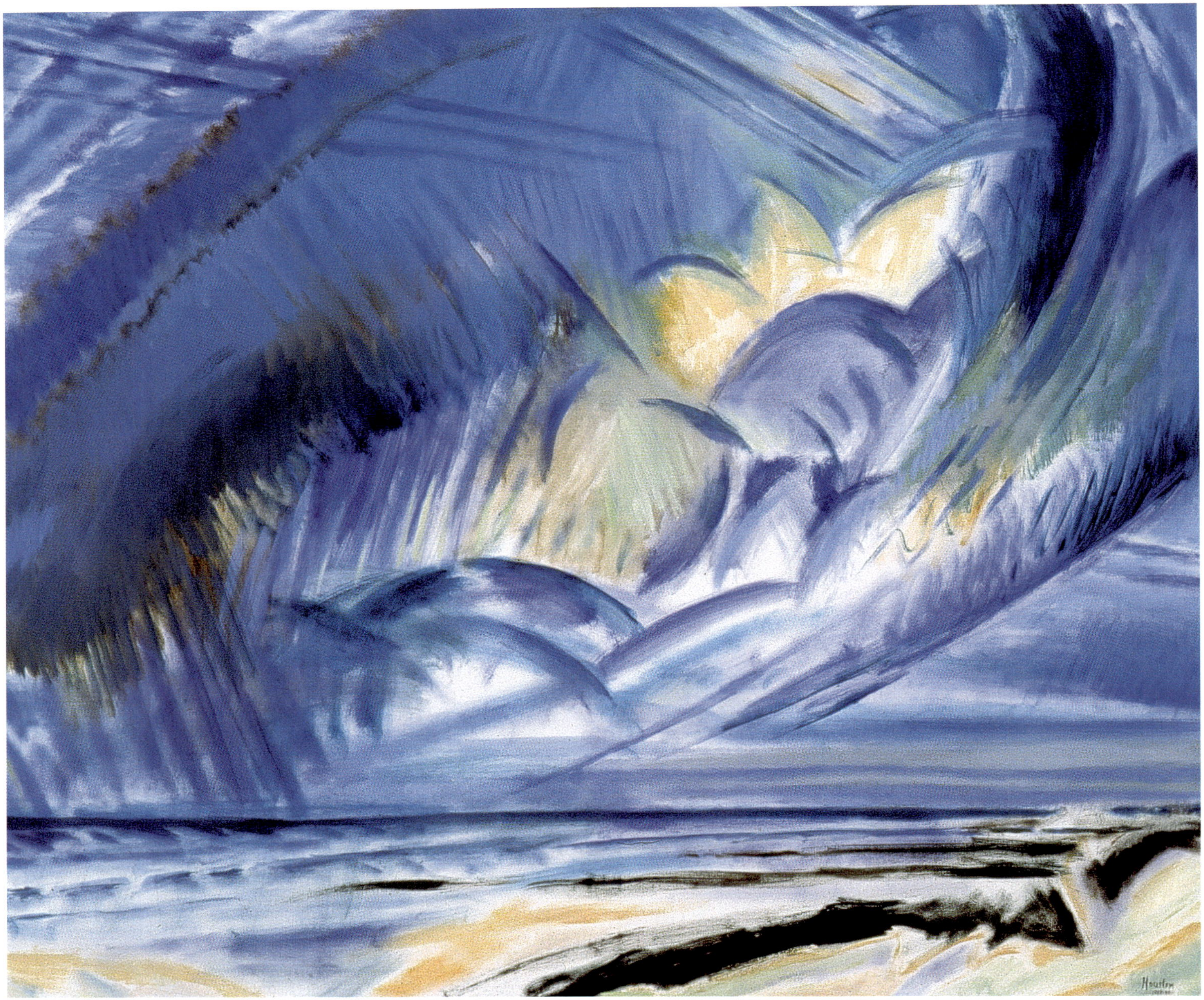

for working in the studio, even though you also work on a small scale in the studio?

Yes, I'm not a very direct painter.

— *What do you mean by 'direct'?*

I mean going outside and painting the subject straight away. I usually make one statement, and then it tends to dry out. I feel I can operate when there's something up there on the canvas that I can refer to, work on or retain. In certain cases I like one colour to dry and then lay another on top; this, as opposed to the very direct kind of painting which you have to employ outside. With watercolour, physically and technically I seemed to be able to cope outside; I could get it to do what I was trying to achieve more readily than I could with oil. In the last few years most of the work done outside has been smaller in scale than earlier outside work.

— *Do finished paintings relate closely to sketch-book studies, or are the studies part of the process of understanding a subject in preparation for painting in the studio?*

opposite: Shore, Sea and Sky, 1989
Private collection · no.42

right: Winter Walk, 1989–90
Artist's collection · no.43

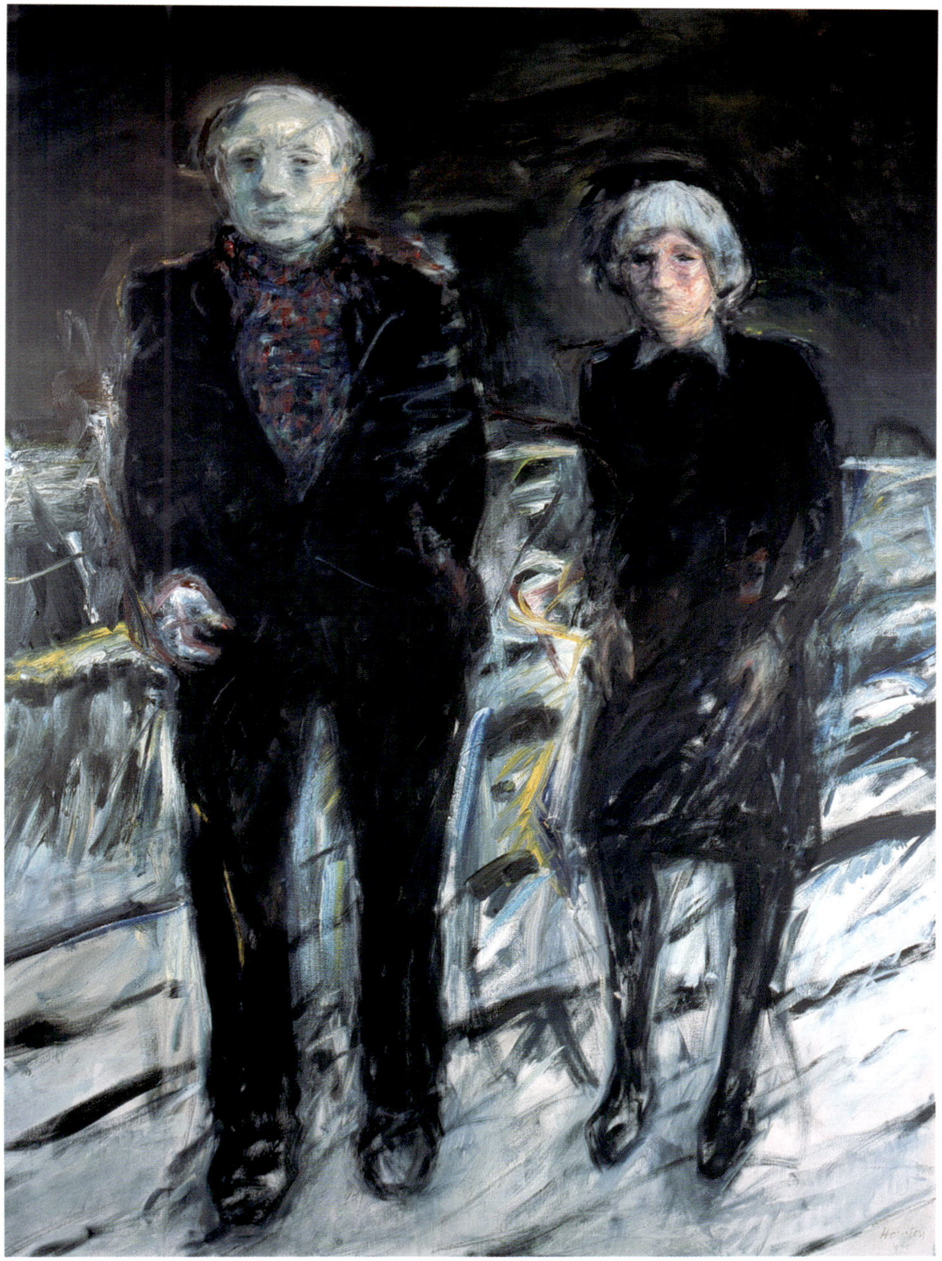

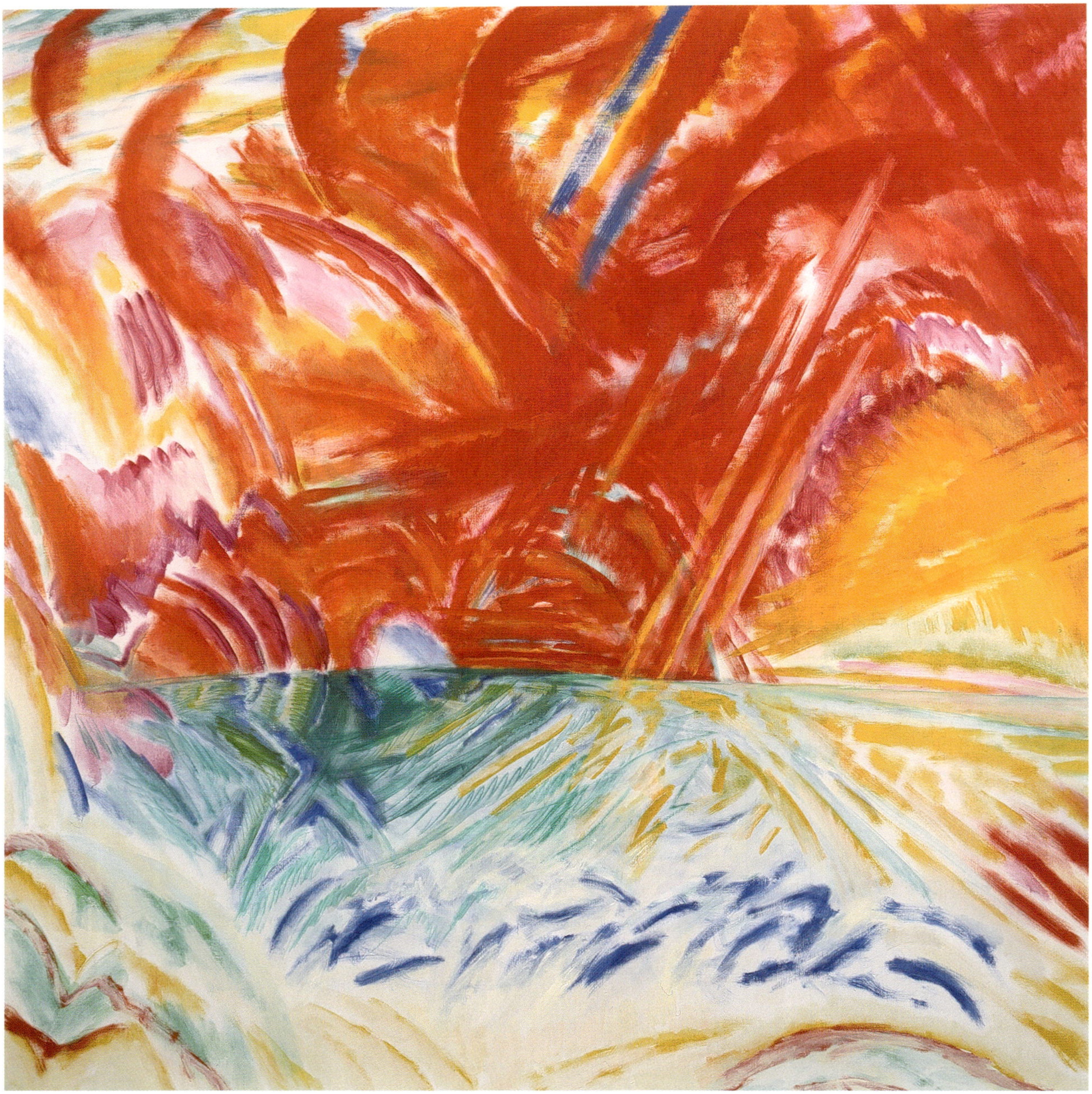

A Day by the Sea, 1990
Artist's collection · no.46

There's a bit of both. Some studies stay as they are. Some are a first statement of an idea, and often it's only at home, when I'm away from the subject, that I remember the essence of the thing. But it means I'm provided with a study – I use pencil, pastels and watercolours when working outside – of a particular time or quality of light, which is very important to me; I have that to build upon and back up the original idea. But at the same time, and this comes from doing watercolours and from the example of people like Emil Nolde and some of the American painters, things happen on the canvas that I haven't quite planned, but which I become aware of and use. Not mistakes, but as a development from the unthinking start to a painting and the act of just letting things happen. Often the colours on the palette may suggest the painting as much as the first outdoor sketch.

— *So that process of accident is important in how you develop a work?*

Oh yes, because occasionally that has taken me in a more interesting direction than the drawing of the place or person might suggest. But the original drawing remains important; the subject might not be realistically rendered on the canvas, but there would be something of the time of day, or the light, or a rhythm that derives from the sketch. And I go back to the sketch, as it will probably be more structured than the accidents that are happening in the course of the painting. And then there is the accident of what colours I squeeze out. I've liked ranges of colours at particular times of my life, and often that dictates the subject.

— *You paint landscape, often the same landscape, in a great variety of ways, and the works appear to express different moods. Is that word 'mood' important to you?*

I think so. That's one of the things I will probably take away in memory from a subject – the light and the mood. The mood will be caught up with light, certain things to do with the time of day, the weather and so on. And that is something I would probably retain in the studio, maybe more than being truthful to the sketch as far as the physical nature of things might be. I might make the Bass Rock a lot smaller to create the feeling of space. I might make the curve of a beach more curved, again for the structure; but something which always remains is that first mood. I'll do a whole lot of sketches from the original sketches. I might make certain features or colours more dominant for the mood or the light of the composition. I might marry a sky showing one particular form of clouds into another picture, which might show the sea under different conditions. I then have to fuse the light and the colour, but I'm able to do that from various sketches of different places.

— *Are you particularly aware of an overall style in your paintings? Your work has been referred to as expressionistic, and part of a Scottish tradition in this – does this description mean anything to you?*

I know I've been described as an expressionistic painter. I suppose I'm sympathetic to other expressionist painting. Quite a few Scottish artists have been interested in artists like Munch, Soutine, Nolde, Beckman, Kirchner and so on. At the same time a lot of the painters I have known have admired Picasso, Braque, Bonnard, Vuillard, Morandi and Klee. Looking back to Giotto, you can see the expressionism in his series of paintings in Assisi – the angels, the crying faces, the movements and gestures of the hands. Even though I admire Piero della Francesca a great deal, for me, his work doesn't have the drama and expression found in a Giotto or a Masaccio. In my paintings I think I cold-bloodedly work and plot them, but somewhere along the line I usually lose my temper with them and rely a great deal on using this emotion intuitively, thinking something has to be done and whatever it is, it's going to be better than what's there.

— *So losing your temper is a productive energy?*

Yes, particularly when the work feels as if it has become too pretty, too planned. That, I suppose, is where the expression is for some painters; even though you've worked it out, eventually you do not want too much planning or thought to get in the way of the mood and feeling you are trying to create. That usually happens in most of my paintings, whether large or very small. I have to take a chance, and I destroy a lot, usually by painting over them and getting them going again. I remember when I first started teaching I shared a class with William MacTaggart. He was talking about painting and said, 'I hate painting on a blank canvas; I can't operate until there is something else there.' Now I can see what he was thinking, though I didn't quite understand at the time.

— *Finally, the Scottish landscape dominates as a subject in your painting. Is there something about that landscape that you feel is particularly important to your work?*

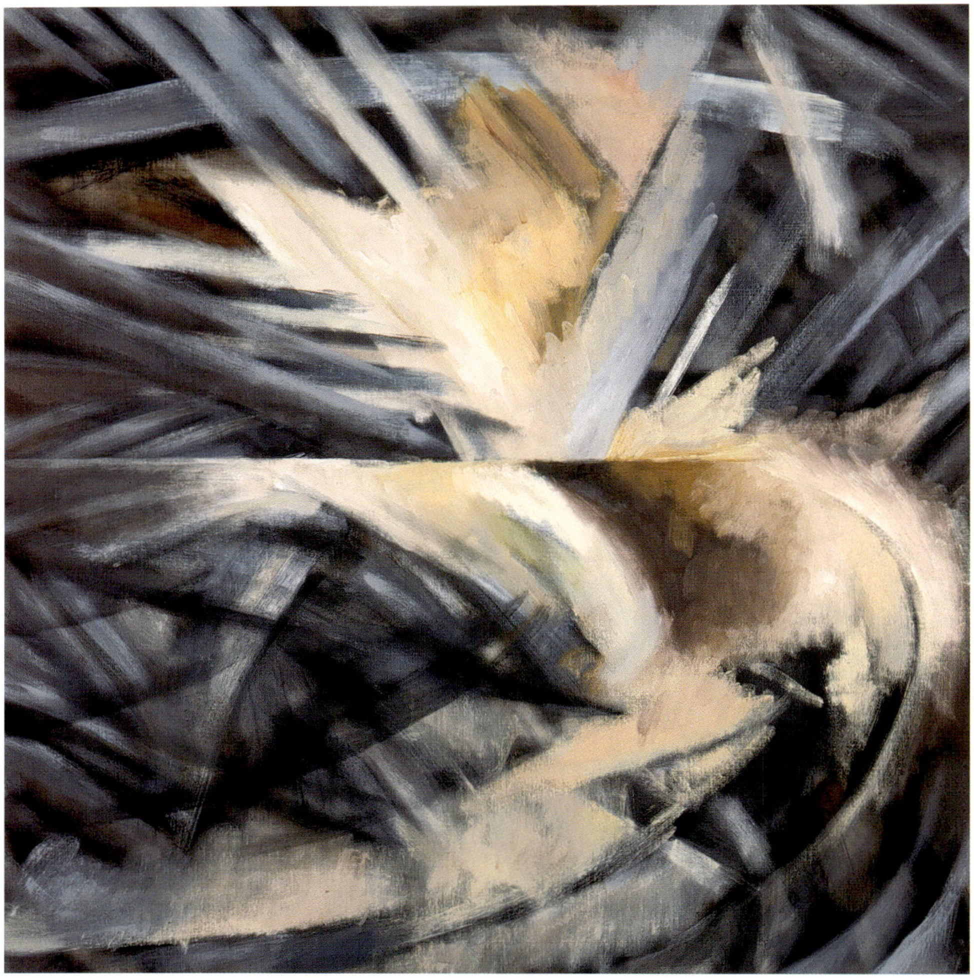

Bay after Storm, 1990
Fleming-Wyfold Art Foundation, London · no.45

It's the landscape I grew up with and know best, so it seems a natural subject to choose. I've no interest in the idea of it being Scottish, or that this is Scotland in any nationalistic sense. This is where I happen to paint and was brought up. Because I know it and see it all the time, I can hang different ideas on it. Also, Britain, being an island, is useful as the weather changes constantly, and that suits a painter like me. Different light and weather effects are stimulants to me; I respond to them and they set me off. We've travelled regularly to Harris, Arisaig and Caithness, and all have been productive. It's often on the second visit that I see something meaningful. Very rarely has it happened on a first visit. Familiarity makes you see past the obvious.

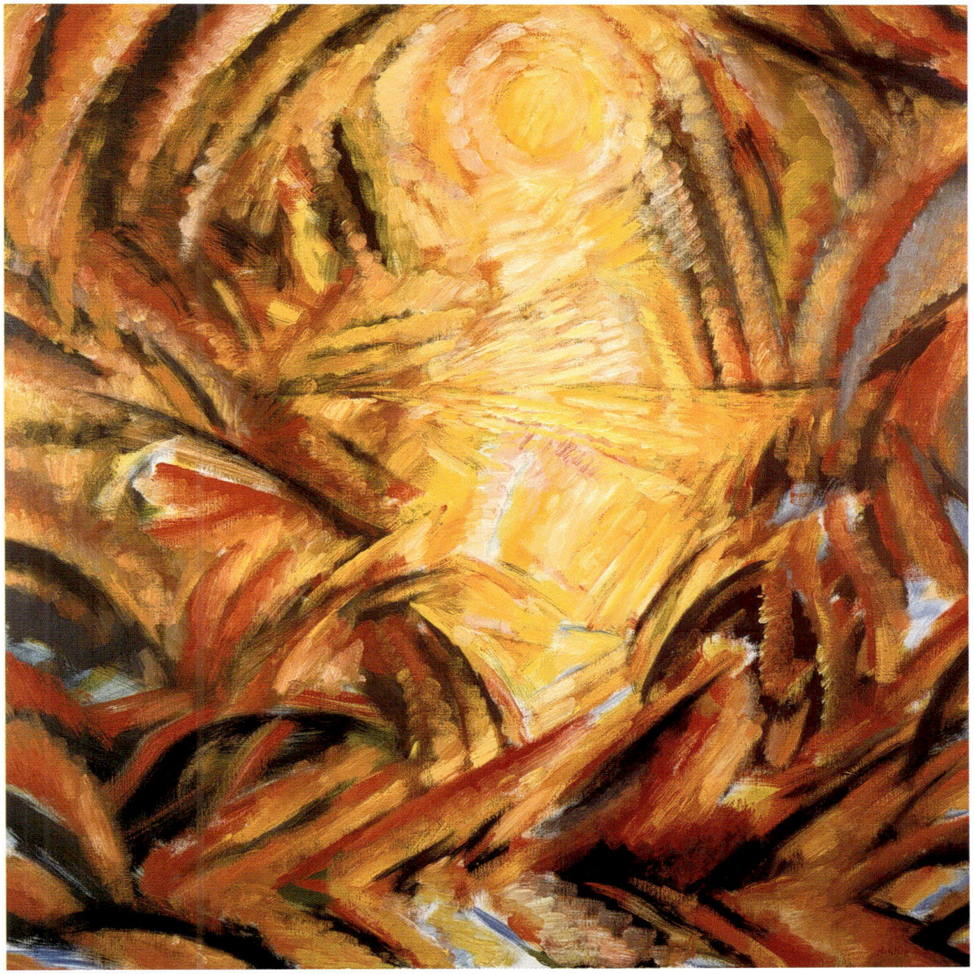

Path to the Fields, Autumn, 1990

Artist's collection · no.44

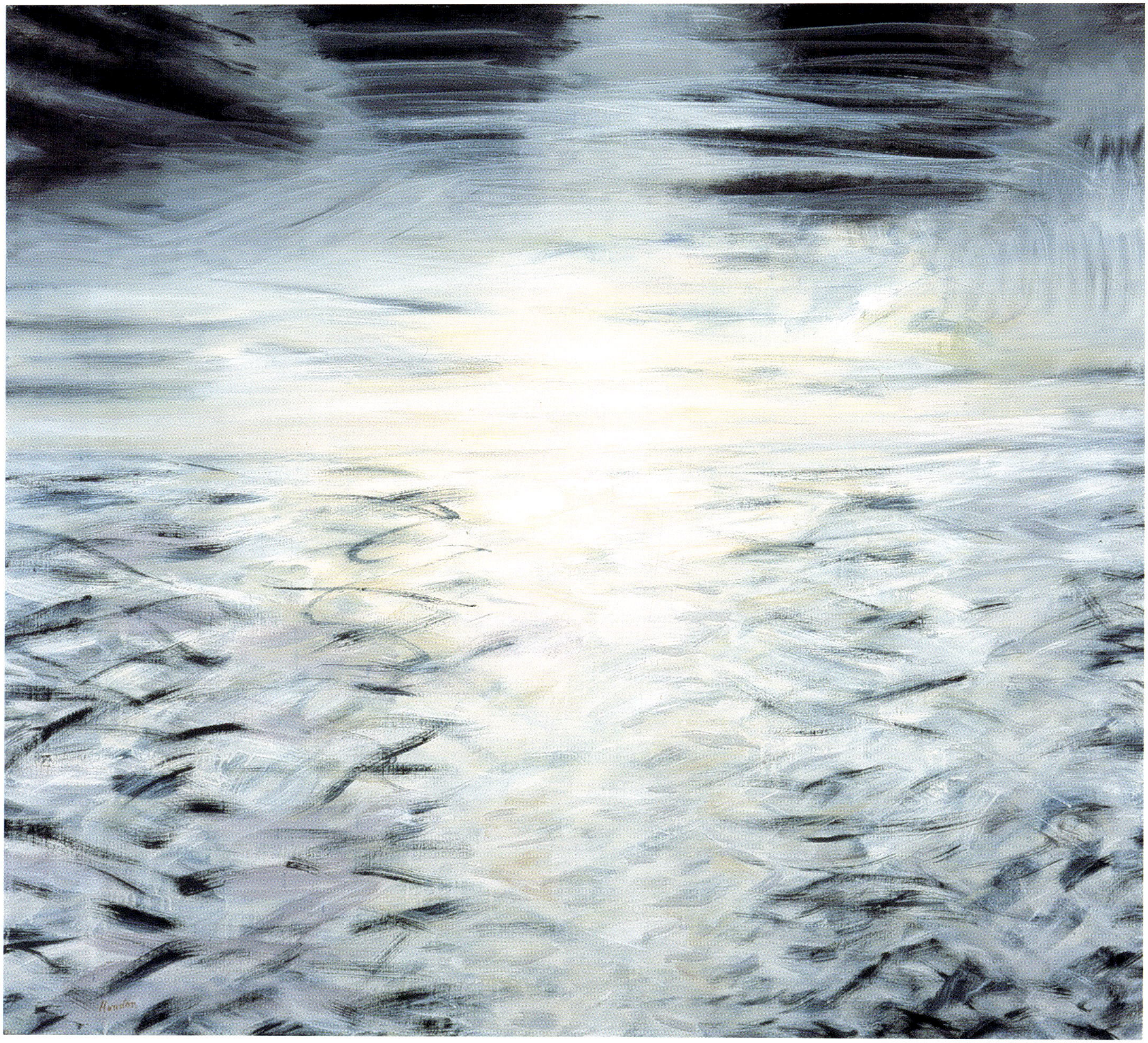

above: Grand Canal Series no.8, 2002–3

The Governor and Company of the Bank of Scotland · no.54

opposite: Light on the Sea, 1999–2000

Artist's collection · no.52

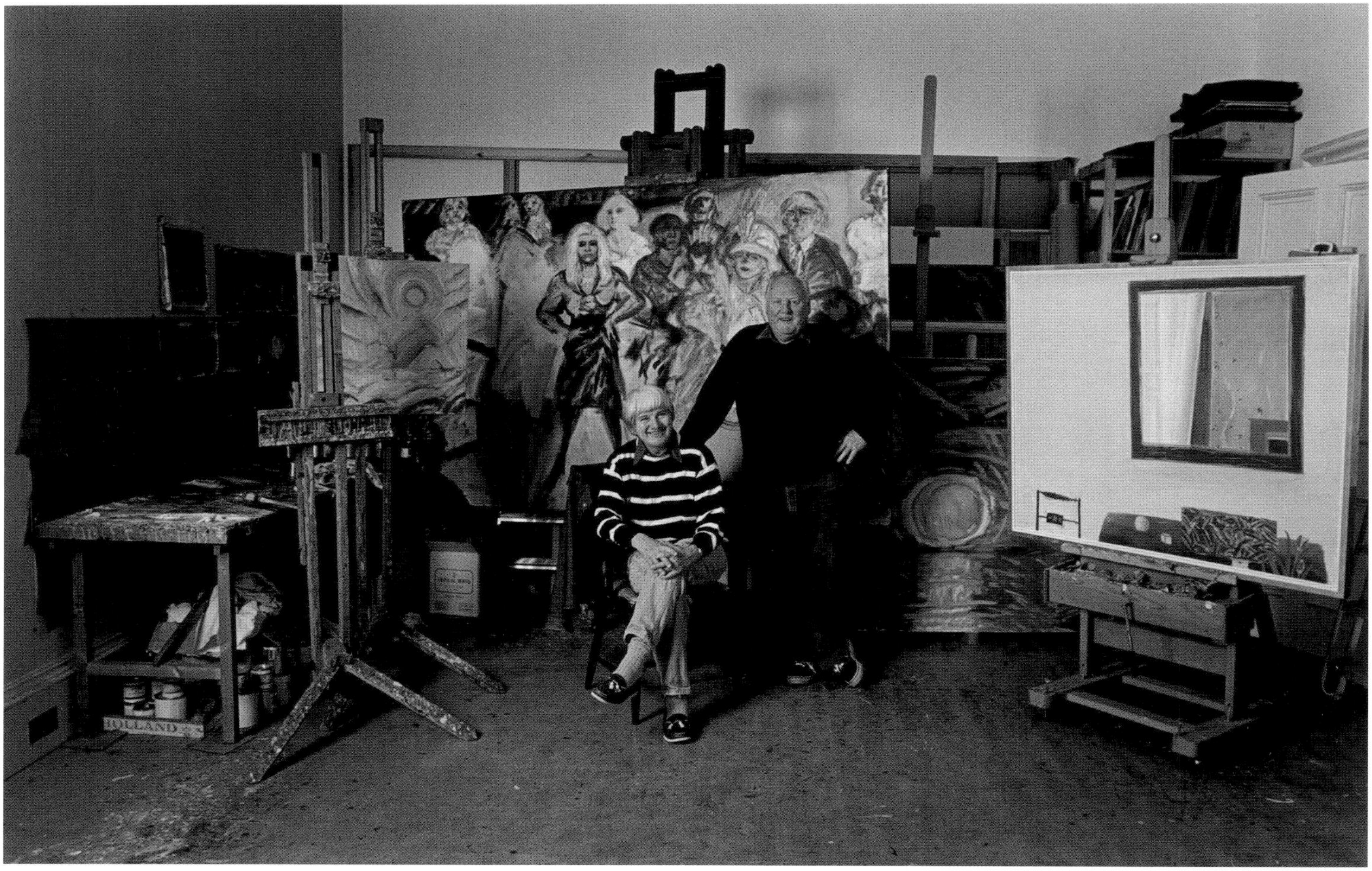

John Houston and Elizabeth Blackadder
at home in Edinburgh, *c.*1984
Artist's collection

Chronology and selected exhibitions

1930
Born 1 April in Buckhaven, Fife.

1948–52
Studied at Edinburgh College of Art.

1952
Awarded an Andrew Grant postgraduate scholarship, allowing a further year's study at Edinburgh College of Art. Elected to the Society of Scottish Artists.

1953
Awarded an Edinburgh College of Art travelling scholarship. Travelled to Italy together with fellow student David Michie, staying from October 1953 to March 1954.

1954–5
Undertook teacher training at Moray House College of Education, Edinburgh. Taught briefly in a Fife primary school. Visited Italy, Yugoslavia and Greece with Elizabeth Blackadder.

1955
Appointed part-time teacher at Edinburgh College of Art. Work commissioned by Shell Petroleum Co. Ltd, and included in their exhibition, *Artists' View of an Industry*, London, and tour through Europe.

1956
Married Elizabeth Blackadder. Moved to 7 London Street, Edinburgh (the artist Anne Redpath lived in the same block). Included in the exhibition, *Industrial Britain*, Chenil Gallery, London.

1957–8
Visited Paris, Barcelona and Madrid. First solo exhibition, at the 57 Gallery, Edinburgh.

1959
Elected to the Royal Scottish Society of Painters in Watercolour.

1960
First solo exhibition with The Scottish Gallery, Edinburgh. Subsequent exhibitions held there in 1962, 1965, 1967, 1971, 1975, 1980, 1990, 1993, 1997 and 2003.

1963
Received Guthrie Award, Royal Scottish Academy. Included in *Fourteen Scottish Painters*, Commonwealth Institute, London; *Contemporary Scottish Painting*, Arts Council of Great Britain touring exhibition of England.

1965
Received Cargill Prize, Royal Glasgow Institute (shared with Ceri Richards). Included in *Contemporary Scottish Painters*, Glynn Vivian Art Gallery, Swansea and Scottish National Gallery of Modern Art; *Seven Scottish Painters*, IBM Gallery, New York.

1966
Included in the inaugural exhibition of the Richard Demarco Gallery, Edinburgh. First solo exhibition with the Mercury Gallery, London. Subsequent exhibitions held there in 1968, 1970, 1972, 1975, 1977, 1979, 1981, 1983 (in Edinburgh), 1984, 1985 (in Edinburgh), 1989, 1992, 1995, 1998 and 2000.

1967
Included in *Fifteen British Artists*, Museum of Modern Art, Warsaw.

1968
Included in *Three Centuries of Scottish Painting*, National Gallery of Canada, Ottawa.

1969
First visit to United States. Artist in residence at the Prairie School, Racine, Wisconsin. Exhibition with Ben Shahn, at the Johnson Foundation, Racine.

1970
Exhibition with the Cerberus Gallery, New York. Included in *Twelve Scottish Painters*, Maine State Commission on the Arts and Humanities (touring exhibition of the United States and Canada).

1971
Included in *The Edinburgh School*, Edinburgh College of Art.

1972
Elected Academician of the Royal Scottish Academy.

1974
Retrospective exhibition, Glen Pavilion, Dunfermline (Fife County Council Education Committee).

1975
Moved to 57 Fountainhall Road, Edinburgh.

1976
With Patrick Caulfield and Glen Onwin included in the inaugural exhibition of the Eden Court Theatre, Inverness. Solo exhibition, Gaelic College, Skye (Scottish Arts Council).

1978
Included in *Painters in Parallel*, Scottish Arts Council/Edinburgh College of Art.

1980
Included in *Master Weavers. Tapestries from the Dovecot Studios*, Scottish Arts Council Festival Exhibition, Royal Scottish Academy, Edinburgh.

1983
Appointed deputy head of the School of Drawing and Painting, Edinburgh College of Art.

1986
First visit to Japan. Commissioned by the Scottish National Portrait Gallery to paint portrait of Sir Alexander Gibson. Included in *British Artists and the Sea 1900–1986*, Laing Art Gallery, Newcastle-upon-Tyne.

1987
Works on Paper, Talbot Rice Gallery, University of Edinburgh (toured to Aberdeen Art Gallery and Maclaurin Art Gallery, Ayr). *Prints and Painting* (with Elizabeth Blackadder), Glasgow Print Studio.

1988
Commissioned by British Rail to produce large mural for Eglinton Station, Glasgow.

1989
Retired from Edinburgh College of Art. Included in *Scottish Art since 1900*, Scottish National Gallery of Modern Art, and Barbican Art Gallery, London (1990). Window design commissioned by the National Library of Scotland.

1990
Awarded OBE.

1991
Included in *Scottish Art in the 20th Century*, Royal West of England Academy, Bristol.

1993
Included in *Scottish Painting*, Flowers East, London.

1999
Exhibition of monoprints at Glasgow Print Studio. Included in *Liberation and Tradition. Scottish Art 1963–75*, Aberdeen Art Gallery and McManus Galleries, Dundee; *Seven Scottish Painters*, Solomon Gallery, Dublin.

2000
Included in *Artists at Harleys*, Hunterian Art Gallery, University of Glasgow.

2002
Included in *160th Anniversary Exhibition*, The Scottish Gallery, Edinburgh.

2004
Solo exhibition at Browse and Darby, London. Awarded honorary degree, Heriot Watt University, Edinburgh.

2005
Exhibition, *John Houston & Elizabeth Blackadder*, City Art Centre, Edinburgh. Awarded honorary degree, Aberdeen University.

List of works

Dimensions are given in centimetres, height before width. Unless otherwise indicated, works are in the collection of the artist.

1 Wellsgreen Pit, 1949
Ink on paper · 17.7 x 22.7

2 Methil Docks, 1951
Ink on paper · 17.3 x 11.2

3 Methil Docks, 1951
Ink on paper · 17 x 22.8

4 Wellsley Pit, 1951
Pencil on paper · 25.5 x 20.5

5 Miner, 1951
Ink and wash on paper · 24.6 x 14.7

6 St Monance, 1952
Gouache and pencil on paper · 20.2 x 25.5

7 Pittenweem, 1951
Goauche on paper · 20.5 x 29.3

8 David Michie in Florence, 1953
Gouache, ink and pencil on paper · 22.9 x 25.7

9 Florence, 1953
Gouache and pencil on paper · 27.7 x 39.2

10 Anticoli, 1954
Pencil on paper · 17 x 22.3

11 Anticoli, 1954
Gouache and watercolour on paper · 19.4 x 26.5

12 Anticoli, 1954
Watercolour and ink on paper · 15 x 19.4

13 Assisi, 1954
Watercolour on paper · 16.7 x 22.1

14 Venice, 1954
Watercolour on paper · 16.7 x 22.1

15 Study after 14th century Virgin and Child, 1954
Charcoal on paper · 40 x 28.5

16 The Tiber Valley, Orvieto, 1954
Gouache on paper · 48.3 x 66

17 Houses, Anticoli, 1954
Gouache on paper · 35.6 x 44.5

18 Hillside, Anticoli, 1954
Ink and gouache on paper · 35.6 x 55.9

19 Winter, Anticoli, 1954
Gouache on paper · 31.8 x 47

20 Two Italian Girls Knitting, Anticoli, 1954
Chalk on paper · 36.8 x 50.8

21 Elizabeth, 1956
Watercolour and pencil on paper · 23.3 x 18.5

22 Cornfields, *c.*1960
Watercolour on paper · 68.6 x 101.6
Scottish National Gallery of Modern Art, Edinburgh: bequeathed by Hazel Heughan, 1993

23 Birds, Flowers and Dark Sun, *c.*1962
Oil on canvas · 86.4 x 112.1
Scottish National Gallery of Modern Art, Edinburgh: purchased, Gulbenkian UK Trust Fund, 1962

24 Village under the Cliffs, 1962
Oil on canvas · 152.4 x 182.9
Scottish National Gallery of Modern Art, Edinburgh: purchased, 1994

25 Evening Sky over the Bass Rock, 1964
Watercolour on paper · 92 x 104

26 Bathers, 1965–6
Oil on canvas · 121.9 x 121.9
Scottish National Gallery of Modern Art, Edinburgh: purchased, 1966

27 Golden Lake II, 1971
Oil on canvas · 123 x 123

28 Sea Sounds, 1971
Oil on canvas · 142.2 x 152.4

29 Stormy Sunset over the Sea, *c.*1972
Oil on canvas · 142 x 152
Royal Bank of Scotland Group Collection

30 Dusk, Harris, 1974
Watercolour on paper · 99 x 60

31 Night Sky, Harris I, 1975
Watercolour on paper · 60 x 99

32 Rainbow over the Sea, Harris, 1975
Watercolour on paper · 65.4 x 99
Elizabeth Blackadder

33 Elizabeth and Cat, 1977
Oil on canvas · 152.4 x 101.6

34 Cliffs, Les Petites-Dalles, 1978–80
Oil on canvas · 127 x 152.4

35 The Yellow Sail, 1980
Oil on canvas · 152.4 x 152.4

36 Three Painters by the Sea (Elizabeth Blackadder, John Bellany, John Houston), 1984
Oil on canvas · 182.9 x 213.4

37 Redhead, New York, 1984
Watercolour on paper · 134 x 79.4

38 Low Tide, North Berwick, 1985
Oil on canvas · 152.4 x 182.9
John Bellany

39 Kyoto, 1987
Oil on canvas · 152.4 x 152.4

40 Elizabeth V, 1987
Watercolour on paper · 94 x 62.2

41 The Bay after the Storm, 1988
Oil on canvas · 152.4 x 182.9
Baring Asset Management Art Collection

42 Shore, Sea and Sky, 1989
Oil on canvas · 152.4 x 182.9
Private collection

43 Winter Walk, 1989–90
Oil on canvas · 243.8 x 177.8

44 Path to the Fields, Autumn, 1990
Oil on canvas · 152.4 x 152.4

45 Bay after Storm, 1990
Oil on canvas · 121.9 x 121.9
Fleming-Wyfold Art Foundation, London

46 A Day by the Sea, 1990
Oil on canvas · 203.2 x 203.2

47 Poppies, 1990
Pencil on paper · 33 x 48.2

48 Shinto Festival, Kyoto, 1994–5
Oil on canvas · 38.1 x 50.8
Private collection

49 Path to a Northern Forest, 1995
Oil on canvas · 121.9 x 121.9

50 Moonlight on the Sea, 1996–7
Oil on canvas · 50 x 61

51 At the Coast, Winter, 1999–2000
Oil on canvas · 152 x 127

52 Light on the Sea, 1999–2000
Oil on canvas · 101.6 x 111.8

53 Sea after Rain, 2002
Pastel on paper · 21 x 22.9
Elizabeth Blackadder

54 Grand Canal Series No.8, 2002–3
Oil on canvas · 91.5 x 91.5
The Governor and Company of the Bank of Scotland

55 Path to the Sea, 2002–3
Oil on canvas · 122 x 122
Private collection

Selected bibliography

Charles Rossner, 'The Artist's View of an Industry', *Printing Review*, autumn 1955

Sydney Goodsir Smith, 'John Houston – a poet in paint', *The Scotsman*, 27 May 1961

T. Elder Dickson, 'Scottish Painting, The Modern Spirit', *Studio International*, December 1963

Emilio Coia, 'Scottish Field', *The Scottish Field*, August 1968

James G. Mowat, *John Houston Retrospective Exhibition* (exhibition catalogue), Fife County Council Education Committee, 1974

Edward Cage, *Edinburgh Ten 30* (exhibition catalogue), Scottish Arts Council / Welsh Arts Council, 1975

Richard Calvocoressi, *John Houston* (exhibition catalogue), Scottish Arts Council / Gaelic College, Skye, 1976

Edward Gage, *The Eye in the Wind: Scottish Painting since 1945*, London: Collins, 1977

Jack Firth, *Scottish Watercolour Painting*, Edinburgh: Ramsay Head Press, 1979

Duncan Macmillan, *John Houston – Works on Paper 1962–87* (exhibition catalogue), Talbot Rice Gallery, University of Edinburgh, 1987

William Packer, *Elizabeth Blackadder – John Houston* (exhibition catalogue), Glasgow Print Studio, 1987

Keith Hartley *et.al.*, *Scottish Art since 1900* (exhibition catalogue), London: National Galleries of Scotland in association with Lund Humphries, 1989

Duncan Macmillan, *Scottish Art 1460–1990*, Edinburgh and London: Mainstream Publishing, 1990

Mary Rose Beaumont, *John Houston* (exhibition catalogue), The Scottish Gallery, 1990

Bill Hare, *Contemporary Painting in Scotland*, New York: Craftsman House, 1992

Duncan Macmillan, *Scottish Art in the 20th Century*, Edinburgh and London: Mainstream Publishing, 1994

Iain Gale, 'Force of Nature', *Scotland on Sunday*, 10 August 1997

Christopher Allan, *Artists at Harleys* (exhibition catalogue), Hunterian Art Gallery, University of Glasgow, 2000

William Packer, *John Houston*, Aldershot: Lund Humphries, 2003

Photographic Credits
AIC Photographic Service: nos.16, 19, 33, 34, 39
© Peter Cattrell: p.10
Antonia Reeve: nos.23, 24, 26, 36